D0975554

MARRIED WITHOUT MASKS

MARRIED WITHOUT MASKS

NANCY GROOM

NAVPRESS ◭®

A MINISTRY OF THE NAVIGATORS
P.O. BOX 6000, COLORADO SPRINGS, COLORADO 80934

The Navigators is an international Christian organiza-
tion. Jesus Christ gave His followers the Great Commission to go and make disciples (Matthew 28:19). The aim
of The Navigators is to help fulfill that commission by
multiplying laborers for Christ in every nation.

NavPress is the publishing ministry of The Navigators.
NavPress publications are tools to help Christians grow.
Although publications alone cannot make disciples or
change lives, they can help believers learn biblical discipleship, and apply what they learn to their lives and
ministries.

© 1989 by Nancy Groom
All rights reserved, including translation
Library of Congress Catalog Card Number: 89-61383
ISBN 08910-95632

Printed in the United States of America

FOR A FREE CATALOG OF
NAVPRESS BOOKS & BIBLE STUDIES,
CALL TOLL FREE 800-366-7788 (USA)
or 1-416-499-4615 (CANADA)

CONTENTS

To Bill,
whom I love

AUTHOR

Nancy Groom was a junior high teacher of English and Bible after her graduation from Calvin College in Grand Rapids, Michigan. She married in 1970 and became a full-time mother in 1971. In 1983 she began her career as a free-lance writer and editor of Sunday school, catechism, and Christian day school curriculum materials.

Nancy's leadership in women's Bible studies and support groups over a period of many years has given her wide exposure to the joys and frustrations today's Christian women experience, especially in their marriages. Nancy lives with her husband, Bill, and their teenage son, Christopher, in Miami, Florida.

ACKNOWLEDGMENTS

I wish to thank those who helped make this book possible: To Dr. Allen Curry, my first editor and mentor as a fledgling writer. To Dr. Larry Crabb for the profound influence his seminars and books have had on my personal growth. To my pastor, Steve Brown, who has encouraged me in countless ways, not least of all in my writing. And to Traci Mullins, a perceptive, empathetic editor and cherished colleague.

I am also deeply grateful to my dear friends: To Mary Ann Ulmer, without whose vision and prayers I would never have completed this project. To Lottie Hillard and Robin Reisert, for their invaluable contributions to my manuscript. And to my faithful sisters in Christ who shared their hearts and minds with me as we struggled together to know the Father's pleasure: Joyce, Mari, Melinda, Yvonne, Denise, Victoria, and Catherine.

I am especially indebted to my husband, Bill, and our son, Christopher, whose cooperation made possible the meeting of my deadlines and whose love brings joy to my life.

Finally, I praise the Father for His goodness and faithfulness throughout my journey toward healing.

P · A · R · T

DISCOVERY:
Recognizing the Masks

1

WALKING THE TIGHTROPE:
Striving to Balance Submission and Authority

The tears on Kerri's cheeks traced the outline of her inner pain as she recounted to me her pilgrimage. Middle-aged and attractive, she was facing a crisis in her twelve-year marriage. She had come to share her pain.

Steve courted Kerri delightfully, melting her twenty-seven-year-old heart with his thirty-five-year-old gentle persistence, and the marriage (his second, her first) promised to fulfill all her hopes. She and Steve started off well, and she considered herself happily married. Their two children were much-wanted, and Kerri thrived in her self-chosen role as full-time wife and mother. The entire family was active in a small neighborhood church.

Kerri assumed submission to Steve was a biblical mandate. Because she had always been a strong-willed woman, submission was not easy for her, but she was determined to trust God to shepherd her life through Steve's decisions. Steve liked having a submissive wife, and though he hated making decisions, he capitulated to her expectations—even demands—that he exercise headship in their home.

But Steve's authority was not consistent, swinging to extremes in both directions. Sometimes he bossed her and the children, manipulating them with his anger or silence; at other times he simply retreated, leaving Kerri with the responsibility of making decisions or enforcing discipline with the children. Kerri didn't always know how to be submissive to him.

Eventually, they worked out a system that went like this: When a decision had to be made (about a vacation, about tithing, about the children, about anything of consequence), Kerri would say, "Whatever you decide is okay with me, honey." (That was a lie, actually; some decisions would have been decidedly not acceptable to her.) Then Steve would put off the decision and watch for clues about what she really wanted, and that is what he would "decide" to do. He felt that was his safest approach to each situation, and he was let off the hook of feeling responsible if the decision turned out to be a bad one. Steve appeared to be exercising biblical authority and Kerri seemed to be submissive, but after several years of this charade, the underlying animosity between them sometimes gnawed in Kerri's spirit, and a deep anger burned within Steve.

Then came their Terrible Year, unannounced, unexpected, altogether frightening. It began when Kerri joined a recovery group for families of substance abusers. She had grown up in an alcoholic family, and Steve's drinking patterns over their years of marriage had become alarming. The decision, though appropriate, proved disastrous for the relationship.

Steve rebelled in no uncertain terms. His anger, dormant for years, erupted and intensified as she continued her weekly meetings. Gone was the former serenity, however superficial, of their family life. They began to fight openly, accusing and counteraccusing, both of them appalled at their loss of emotional restraint. They pretended to be harmonious when they were with their friends, but both knew better.

Submission was no longer working for Kerri; she did not feel submissive and thought Steve's behavior did not merit her submission. She aligned herself emotionally with her feminist friends because she understood the pain that moves women to "throw off the yoke." Steve's "authority" galled her, and when he exercised it to control her, she could not bring herself to submit to it.

Overcome by increasingly frequent depression, Kerri told me how the night before our talk she had walked through her house, mentally dividing the furniture. She was sure Steve would leave, and she was almost relieved. After a year of terrible turmoil, she had reached the end of her tether. No longer able to hold things together, she was grieving the death of her marriage.

DIFFICULT QUESTIONS

What can be said to the Kerris and Steves of our day? They occupy our divorce courts and our church pews, and sometimes our own homes. They are the women and men who believe a wife's submission to her husband's authority is biblical, but they find themselves unwilling or unable to live out those roles as expected by the Christian community. Wanting to please the Father and yet live with integrity in their marriages, they are asking weighty questions. Is submission synonymous with obedience? Are submission and self-esteem mutually exclusive? Does authority require a husband to make every family decision? Is exercising authority the same as bossing? If a woman's husband is an unbeliever or refuses to assume godly headship, must she still submit to him? If so, how?

What option does a husband have if his wife refuses to submit to or acknowledge his headship? May he force her submission? How should a godly woman act when her husband demeans or abuses her, and how should a godly man respond to his wife's public criticism? What about their negative emotions? Can they simply choose to not feel angry or unhappy? Is there a "right" way to exercise submission and authority?

The words *submission* and *authority* are fraught with emotional overtones and are likely to elicit a broad spectrum of reactions from individuals. While I was writing this book, people often asked about my topic, and when I told them, inevitably a sort of uncomfortable silence followed. Few Christian husbands or wives remain neutral about these words. Either they defend the concepts as scriptural and try to live them out, or they resist them and interpret Scripture's "submission passages" as being relevant only to the first-century communities to which Paul and Peter wrote.

Particularly in today's culture in which women are demanding liberation, the Church must struggle to remain true to biblical principles and yet interpret a wife's submission and a husband's authority in a way that allows both to exercise their giftedness in God's service. Submission and authority must be painted in both biblical and contemporary hues, or the Church will have missed its calling to make relevant the eternal verities of Scripture.

THE LEVELS OF A MARRIAGE

Foundational to understanding the wrong patterns of submission and authority practiced in many Christian marriages is the realization that every marriage lives, so to speak, on three levels. Steve and Kerri's marriage, for example, exists as a public marriage, a family marriage, and an internal relationship inside each partner. These three tiers of a particular marital relationship are often strikingly dissimilar. The way the public evaluates that marriage may be far more positive—or negative—than the family's assessment. And the couple's inner judgment of how the relationship is faring may differ from both the public image and the family image.

Public Level

The public image describes the marital relationship that the partners show to the world—to friends, church members, business associates, and social acquaintances. Many couples work hard to project the best possible image when they are in public. I can remember times when I was dying on the inside because of a cutting remark my husband, Bill, had made on the way to church, but we smiled and spoke pleasantly to each other once we arrived. We were deeply committed to looking good, especially at church. When others saw us as the perfect couple, that was exactly what we wanted them to see. No one got a clue from us that there was anything wrong. We carefully maintained our marriage's public image.

Family Level

A second level of marriage is the at-home or family relationship between husband and wife. It is the marriage the children might see; it is also the relationship as the partners perceive and verbalize it to each other. At this level the spouses develop their own relational styles and live out the good and bad of married life. They deal more or less successfully with money, the house, the children, daily meals, love-making, vacations—all the decisions and actions that make up their days. This level of the marriage is usually more honest, more real, than the public image the couple projects away from home. Without the need to impress others, especially the Christian community, both spouses express more of who they really are to each other.

Of course, each partner may perceive the marriage differently. For example, the husband may think everything is fine while the wife is beginning to notice some serious problems developing. Or she may think her words and actions make him feel valued and respected, but he actually feels unappreciated.

For the first several years of my marriage, I considered myself a wonderful submissive wife—until a good friend pointed out how I was undermining Bill's confidence by continually questioning his decisions. I thought we were doing fine, but my friend knew better than either of us.

If husband and wife can communicate honestly with each other, they will be more likely to agree on how good or bad things are. At any rate, the at-home level of the marriage is separate from—and often different from—its public image. Too often the news of the latest divorce elicits an amazed response of "Who, *them*? Who would have suspected *they* were having trouble?"

Inner Level

A marriage has more to it than its public and private sides, however. A third and deeper level is the inner, often unexamined life of the marriage—the emotions and thoughts each partner has about the other. Individuals really live as husbands and wives in this hidden aspect of the relationship. What is said, or often only felt, deep inside about a spouse indicates the real health or illness of the marriage, regardless of how it looks to the public or to the children or even externally to each partner.

Sometimes, the unseen dynamic in the relationship is hidden even from the marriage partners themselves. For whatever reasons, one or both may be unable or unwilling to look honestly at true feelings about the other. Fearing—consciously or unconsciously—that their feelings may not be positive, they choose to work hard at polishing up the exterior of their public or family marriage in hopes that the inner discontent will somehow diminish or disappear altogether.

Bill and I made geographical moves almost every year for the first six years of our marriage, and I became expert at packing and labeling boxes. During our last move, I discovered boxes we had never unpacked; we'd just carried them from place to place and never looked inside. We've done that with some of our problems, too—carrying them around without ever facing and solving them.

Often it seems too scary or overwhelming to deal with what is really going on inside. A couple may attend marriage seminars on communication or read books about fair marital fighting, yet they remain untouched at the center of their beings by the one to whom they are covenantally related. Though they hate to admit it and sometimes refuse to admit it, even to themselves, they are lonely in their marriages and don't have the faintest idea what to do about it.

AUTHORITY AND SUBMISSION AT THE THREE LEVELS

How, then, should we talk about submission and authority in the light of these levels of marriage? If God calls for a balance of authority and submission in the marital relationship, at what level should it happen? Does God want a Christian husband to demonstrate his authority and his wife to behave submissively when they are in public? Surely it matters to some degree what others say about our marriages if we are called to be God's ambassadors in every phase of life. And how about authority and submission at home? Is it required even when no one else—including the children—is aware of what is being said or done between husband and wife? Finally, what about the inner life of the marriage? Does God's Word mandate submission and authority there, too? Or is it okay to follow the example of the rambunctious kindergartner restricted to his chair who announced, "I'm sitting down on the outside, but inside I'm standing up"?

Another question to consider is this: Do submission and authority look the same at all three levels? Might there be an opinion or a needed rebuke that a wife would choose not to say to her husband in public but only in the quiet of their living room? Should he confront her lack of responsiveness to his leadership in front of the children? Must a wife's inner spirit toward the marriage always align with the submission she chooses to act out in public or at home? And is a husband to always live out his true inner feelings toward his wife?

MARRIAGE MASKS

Part of Kerri and Steve's problem was that her submission and his exercise of authority were mere masks behind which they were living. They were unaware of the many dynamics they had brought into the marriage and the accumulated experience of twelve years of living together. Kerri was right to believe that submission is biblical, but she failed to examine her "submissive" behavior or to look at why she was submitting to Steve. And Steve was right to believe that God had given him the responsibility to exercise authority in his home, but he never bothered to critically consider how or why he was doing it.

The unexamined issues of their lives remained unresolved. Kerri was not investigating her longing to be valued as a woman, her deep fear of disapproval and rejection, and her driving need to control the people and circumstances of her life. Steve was not facing his fear of criticism, his deep sense of inadequacy as a husband and father, and his urgent need to keep his wife under his control. These were the hidden aspects of Steve and Kerri's submission-authority pattern that revealed themselves only when the trauma of marital crisis forced them to review their lives and their marriage.

USEFUL PRETENSE

Several years ago I sang in a large church choir that regularly planned fun things to do together. Every Halloween, for example, choir members came to rehearsal in costumes and enjoyed a party afterward. One year almost the entire second-alto section—twelve of us in all—dressed as clowns. We were painted and costumed at the home of a semiprofessional clown, and as he made up our faces, he said we would feel like different people with masks to hide behind. We would sense a freedom to do what we would not normally do unmasked. He was right. My clown makeup served a dual purpose, protecting my real identity and projecting a desired image to other choir members. The paint and costume let me be a different me for a while, and it was fun.

The masks we wear as husbands and wives serve us in similar ways, protecting and projecting. Submissive behavior can protect a wife from revealing her deep inner hurt and fear, keeping her safe from being known and possibly rejected. It can also project an image she wishes others to see and believe, an image of godliness and obedience she may not really be experiencing. A husband's mask of authority may protect him from the uncertainty he feels about his adequacy, and at the same time it may project an image of strength and control he wants others to think he has. The persons behind the masks get to be—or at least appear—different from what they really are.

Usually, the masks are worn unconsciously. Steve and Kerri's earlier relationship, for example, was not a deliberate charade. She unconsciously hid behind a mask of submission, and it served her well by keeping her safe from certain personal realities for many years. Steve's mask of authority maintained in him a false sense of mastery over his world so that he didn't have to look honestly at his style of leadership with Kerri and the children.

Both were unaware of their own masks, and neither recognized the other's mask. Their games were unannounced and unacknowledged. Their ideas about submission and authority in marriage had been rooted in a mutual desire to behave biblically, but because those concepts were unexamined, they were misunderstood and wrongly practiced by both partners.

A marriage as it appears on the public level is often a well-constructed facade of marital compatibility hiding tumultuous feelings of bitterness and discontent—feelings that are sometimes unacknowledged by one or both partners. And because it is possible for actions *not* to express an inward reality, making changes in external behavior is simply not enough when considering what to do about the problems in intimate relationships.

We must look beneath the surface of our marriages and ask some complex questions: Why is it so difficult for a woman to submit to her husband? Why does a husband need so desperately to assert his authority? Why do we all wear masks instead of being open and vulnerable in our marriages? What patterns might there be in each of us that make us conform outwardly to a standard we inwardly rebel against? In what ways do these patterns affect us? Why are we so afraid to change? Why does a woman sometimes experience so much (often unspoken) anger, even when she thinks she is doing all the correct submissive things? And why do so many husbands struggle with both their desire for and their terror of being the leader God has called them to be?

THE STRUGGLE FOR INTEGRITY

These questions reach to the heart of where we live in the inner tiers of our marriages. Often a wife can evidence submissive behavior on the public level, and perhaps even on the private level to some extent. But most women strive desperately to acquire inner submission, which God asks for at the deepest level of our living if we are to submit "as unto the Lord."

This inner submission, if it is honestly examined, is the point at which the struggle for integrity is waged in the souls of most women. Often, for a variety of reasons, a woman is asked to sacrifice more than she should in the name of submission to her husband's authority. Then the "oughts" and expectations hinted at or openly taught by the Christian community wreak havoc with her conscience. If she reacts to the pressure by trying more diligently to act out the submissive role, she may succeed in pleasing other Christians and/or her husband. But she may also end up feeling that her gifts are being wasted and that she is losing a sense of who she is as a created and redeemed image-bearer of God. All too often such a woman eventually comes to resent the God who she believes called her to that (wrong) kind of submission.

Christian men struggle with their authority role, too. They know God has called them to headship in their families, and many try to project a public image of strength and confidence. Yet despite their often successful leadership in the business or professional world (and even in the church), many of those same men live in fear of the headship God requires in their intimate relationships. Often they feel inadequate to the task.

Bluffing their way (by playing the macho role, for example) leaves their anxiety unresolved and their wives unresponsive, but retreating from family leadership is no solution, either. On the inner level of their lives, many husbands simply do not know how to experience the competence that would allow them to lead their wives without bullying them, to love without intimidating or neglecting them. All too often when it comes to family headship, husbands feel stuck with an impossible task they can neither accomplish nor ignore.

It is time to reexamine the entire issue of submission and seek to create a marital environment in which a woman can submit and her husband can lead without either one having to sacrifice integrity. We must focus on some serious questions as we walk toward maturity and greater intimacy with God and with the people who inhabit our lives. They are not comfortable questions, and answering them will be disruptive, both internally and externally.

When we face the mess within, the life without becomes confused, unpredictable, and risky. Asking questions is unsettling, and Christians who like things neat and clear-cut will probably want to avoid the process altogether. Those who expect to be told what submissive things to do or what steps of authority to take in order to fix what's wrong in their marriage will be disappointed—even angry—about having to struggle for answers in the complex world of dynamic marital relationships.

But the struggle has its rewards. Though Kerri and Steve could not recognize it in the midst of their pain, their Terrible Year was potentially a wonderful blessing. The Father had their best interest in mind when He brought them to the point where they had to change because their masks no longer worked for them. It was time for them to grow up in their marriage and honestly evaluate the motives behind their behavior. The crises that have unsettled my marriage in recent years are, in retrospect, a part of God's blueprint for bringing Bill and me to Himself for genuine healing.

Surface living has never been God's intention for His image-bearers; He wants us to learn to live a new way, unprotected by our masks. As awful as that unsettling year was for Steve and Kerri, it offered them the possibility of beginning a new life with a deeper and more open relationship with God and with each other.

SUMMING UP

Many Christian husbands and wives are struggling with these and similar issues. They are fed up with surface spirituality and artificial answers. They recognize how much effort is required to balance their desire for intimacy with their need to know themselves mutually strong in their marriages, and they are tired of playing it safe. Desiring to obey the biblical mandates of submission and authority, Christian marriage partners often sense that they have been doing it the wrong way and for the wrong reasons far too long. They want to restore a balance of respect and love in their marriages, but they are not sure how to do it. Being both biblical and content with the submission-authority principle in marriage requires courage to honestly look within and a willingness to change old thought and behavior patterns.

The tightrope between personal competence and appropriate dependence in a marriage relationship is not easy for a woman to walk. And a husband's balancing of responsible strength and loving involvement with his wife and family is no simple task. Yet that is our opportunity as Christian marriage partners. We are called to godly submission and an exercise of self-sacrificing authority.

What does that mean, and how can we pull it off? Those are the questions of the hour. Husbands and wives who are courageous enough to face their hidden motives, take responsibility for their spiritual maturing, and invest the time required to change old habits can learn to live as God intended. They can be married without masks.

QUESTIONS FOR THOUGHT AND DISCUSSION

1. How did Kerri fail to act biblically toward Steve?

2. In what ways did Steve not behave biblically toward Kerri?

3. Describe your feelings when you think about a wife's submission to her husband.

4. Explain what *submission* means to you.

5. Why do you think a woman should or should not submit to her husband if he doesn't deserve it?

6. Give reasons for your agreement or disagreement with your church's teaching about submission.

7. Choose a marriage relationship you know well, perhaps your own, and evaluate it on each level: public, family, and inner.

8. If you are married, identify one aspect of your style of relating to your spouse that could be considered a mask.

C·H·A·P·T·E·R

2

BAROMETRIC PRESSURE:
Submission as Absorption

The mood was quietly reflective as several in the group of about two dozen Christians talked about their inappropriate ways of relating to the substance abusers in their families.

Suzanne spoke up: "I've always let John be sort of my barometer. If he's doing fine, so am I. But if he's using drugs or is in a terrible mood, I feel awful, and my life seems totally out of control."

Nick, the father of an alcoholic daughter, nodded in understanding, then added, "It's so ridiculous, isn't it? If someone called on the phone to ask how I was doing, I'd probably turn to my daughter and ask her how she's doing, then give *her* answer to the person who called. I'm always taking her emotional temperature so I'll know what my own is! I've become so absorbed in taking care of her, so afraid she'll fall apart, I've lost track of myself."

What had begun as a legitimate concern for loved ones had deteriorated over time into something quite different. Gradually, Suzanne and Nick shifted from caring about their family members to taking responsibility for their happiness. In the process, the caretakers lost sight of their own needs and feelings, focusing all their energy on the substance abusers' chaotic existence. The end result was a kind of absorption into the other person's life—a loss of separateness and of individual identity.

Suzanne's and Nick's experience is not uncommon in families struggling with the substance abuse of one member. Everything eventually centers on the emotional condition of the abuser, from whom the entire family takes its cue about what to say and how to act. Every other family member responds primarily to that one person's mood and demands, even when substance abuse is not actually present at the time.

THE BAROMETER SYNDROME

A similar unhealthy emotional dependency is found in other families as well. In many seemingly normal homes one person is caught in a barometer syndrome with another family member. We're not talking here about legitimate empathy. Healthy spouses minister to each other by experiencing and expressing appropriate involvement with each other's joys and sorrows. In a barometer marriage, however, the balance of emotional power is heavily weighted on one side.

In this chapter we will consider primarily the marriage in which the scale tips toward the husband (though sometimes it tips the other way, too). A woman in such a marriage allows her husband great power to set her moods, tastes, preferences, and choices. When he feels good, so does she; when he is upset or angry, she can't keep her own emotional balance. She feels she has to like what he likes, resent what he resents, and (in extreme cases) agree with him about everything.

Some husbands insist on this arrangement and strongly resist any show of independence on the part of their wives, calling it "women's lib" and denouncing it as unChristian. They are deeply invested in staying in charge, often controlling even minute aspects of their wives' lives, such as hairstyle and clothing. Husbands of barometer wives announce, in effect, what they will and will not tolerate, and their wives must "submit" if they are to be considered godly. Though these situations sound extreme, things are often this way in many Christian marriages.

The barometer wife is a woman whose "submission" to her husband masks her absorption into his personality. Her behavior suggests that she is the model of Christian submissiveness, but other issues may be involved. Certainly she occupies the opposite end of the submission spectrum from the wife who vehemently dismisses the entire concept of submission as archaic and repressive. Although the barometer wife may externally (and genuinely) embrace submission as a biblical injunction, an examination of what lies beneath the surface of her life may reveal something quite different from the biblical model of submission. Why, for example, is she not finding her identity in her unique personality and giftedness, her individual strengths and weaknesses, instead of in her husband's accomplishments and personality, his ideas of who she is or should be? Why is she willing to sacrifice her identity to maintain an illusion of intimacy with her husband? Is that really God's design for marriage?

A Christian friend of mine put it this way: "I used to think submission meant that whatever my husband thought, that is what I should do, except for violating the Ten Commandments, of course. I believed I had to lay down my goals, my likes and dislikes, my style, my total person, to minister to him. But I found that it obliterated my own person, and I had nothing left to give of myself."

Another woman said, "In the Christian environment in which I was raised, a woman was expected to give in to her husband's whims and desires—whatever he wanted, really. And if a woman wasn't secure in herself—and most weren't—she just kept on in the same role. I experienced submission as absorption, and it almost destroyed me. I've found it's especially the women who came from Christian backgrounds who get trapped into thinking they must do and be whatever their husbands say in order to feel good about themselves and to keep their husbands happy. Consequently, many ended up being Christian nobodies."

How true. Often, the Christian women who most feel like nobodies on the inside are those trying the hardest to become somebodies in their churches and communities. I, for one, worked hard to make a place for myself without realizing that the driving force behind my "Christian service" was more self-contempt than selflessness. I obligated others to affirm me because I felt so unworthy of their affirmation. I especially needed Bill's approval, yet I thought just being me was never enough. I had to *do*—and *do well*—to deserve his love. So I quit being me and tried to be what he wanted so he wouldn't reject me. I carried his pain and almost lived his life for him. Bill liked caretaking (who wouldn't?) but not the manipulation tha went with it (who would?).

What is going on beneath the surface of a marriage in which the wife allows herself to become simply an extension of her husband, bearing not only his name, but also his very identity Does such a woman know that she has a self of her own? Is it okay foi her to have a self of her own? Can she truly love without a self of her own?

A BAROMETER MARRIAGE

Lorraine is somewhat overwhelmed by her husband. When she met Tom, she was immediately drawn to his strength—so unlike the men she had been used to, especially her father. Tom was decisive, even a little aggressive, and she liked being taken care of and not having to bother about making decisions. She had had enough of decision-making during the two years she had been on her own, working and going to college.

A military man, Tom was fairly attentive to Lorraine, and he was a good provider and a strong disciplinarian with their three children. He prided himself on being a family man (though his bowling league night with "the boys" was not up for debate). He was active in his church, teaching Sunday school and directing the evangelism program. And he insisted that Lorraine and the children be involved in appropriate church activities as well.

Lorraine learned early what Tom liked—his favorite activities, foods, political ideas, even her hair and dress styles—and she found it satisfying to do whatever he wanted. As a Christian, she felt she was modeling the biblical mandate that a wife accommodate herself to her husband. She quickly deferred whenever he exhibited a flash of irritation at her disagreement with something he said or did. Among their friends, and especially within their church community, Tom and Lorraine's relationship was considered the epitome of what a Christian marriage should be.

Except for the usual ups and downs of married life, things ran fairly smoothly for Tom and Lorraine for nineteen years. That was when Lorraine expressed a desire to finish her college degree after their youngest child, Kristen, entered high school. Tom didn't like it. He said, "Why do you need more education when I'm able to provide for you and the children? If you have extra time on your hands, maybe you could volunteer in the church library or at Kristen's school cafeteria."

EVALUATING THIS MARRIAGE

How would you describe Tom and Lorraine's marriage? The barometer marriage usually looks good to the people who view it from the outside. The public image of Tom and Lorraine's marriage generally received a high rating. Some of the military wives considered Lorraine a doormat, but she saw herself as the gentle and quiet woman that the Apostle Peter called Christian wives to be (1 Peter 3:4). Tom was considered a strong leader and responsible head of his family. His pastor wished there were more families like theirs in the church—the "backbone of the congregation," as he would sometimes say.

The family level of this marriage (the way Tom and Lorraine and their family perceived it) also rated relatively high. Tom liked his subdued woman and felt comfortable being in charge, although he didn't always respect Lorraine and at times was frankly rather bored with her. Lorraine found her place safe, thankful that she didn't have to make decisions. Yet her increasingly frequent flashes of resentment toward Tom startled and concerned her when she stopped to think about it. The extended family, their parents and married siblings, thought Tom and Lorraine had a model marriage. Their children were learning that marriage ought to be like the one they observed daily.

But what is really going on underneath, in the inner dynamics of the relationship? Can love flourish when one partner dominates the other? Is that what Paul and Peter meant by submission and authority?

I once asked a group of women, "Do husbands *want* wives who will be absorbed in them?" One woman answered, "Does power feel good?" Someone else countered with, "They may say they want it, but I think they get tired of it, yet don't really know how to change." Tom and Lorraine need to consider what's happening on the inside where they really live.

AN HONEST LOOK WITHIN

What words would Tom use to describe Lorraine to a friend who didn't know her? What does he say secretly to himself that he would never say aloud to anyone about her? He might call her compliant, loving, efficient, dedicated, even obedient. But would he say she was exciting, stimulating, passionate, alive? He might say he was satisfied with their marriage, but there are times (which he tries to ignore) when he is drawn to the women he knows who challenge his opinion and make him think, women who know themselves in a way he thinks Lorraine will never know herself. Deep inside, Tom feels condescending toward Lorraine. When he tries to imagine her being more assertive, though, he retreats into the safety of his familiar expectations of her and reminds himself of how grateful he should be.

How does Lorraine really see her marriage at the below-the-surface level? She might describe Tom to herself as strong, decisive, competent, godly. But would she say he was kind, gentle, involved in her life in a way that deeply touched her? Does she even realize that she wishes he was more tender, more in tune with her inner life? Sometimes she realizes that his almost military discipline of the children has made them more afraid of than close to their father. She senses (though she can't really explain it) a genuine grief for her children's loss, especially as it affects Kristen, their only daughter.

Yet Lorraine is glad to have a strong man to make decisions for her. Her father wasn't very good at that; in fact, he wasn't very involved in her life, either. Whenever Lorraine allows herself to look at her disappointment—with Tom, with her father, with her unrealized dreams of becoming a kindergarten teacher—she just reminds herself that she is lucky to have a man like Tom, and she resolves never to let anyone (least of all Tom) know how she really feels.

That's how things might look beneath the public and family surface of a marriage, which, I suspect, is not uncommon within the Christian community. At the deepest level of the marriage, many things are going on that neither spouse has taken the time to examine. Tom is feeling threatened by Lorraine's legitimate desire for further education and a meaningful job, and she is beginning to realize that she needs more from their relationship than she is experiencing. Lorraine's "submissiveness" over the years has been less a response to God's call for biblical submission and more a way to avoid certain unpleasant realities and hard choices she felt unequipped to handle. In order to genuinely love her husband, she must contemplate what lies beneath her absorption in Tom's life. What does this absorption that is masquerading as submission accomplish for her? For him?

Actually, there is something in it for both of them. Tom benefits from his dominant position by being able to remain uninvolved emotionally in the lives of his wife and children while still retaining a sense of mastery over his world. And Lorraine is invested in her unhealthy dependency because it allows her to avoid responsibility and blame for the events of her life while appearing to the Christian community as a model of submission. Although both benefit from their unbalanced relationship, the benefits are neither healthy nor biblical. Even if there are good and healthy aspects to their relationship, neither Tom nor Lorraine can be said to be truly loving the other one in the right way.

Of course, the submerged dynamics in this marriage are rooted in the events and temperaments that shaped both partners long before their marriage vows were spoken. Both of them brought the baggage of relational habits and self-image into the marriage based on ways they had already learned to relate, particularly to their parents. A teaching colleague once said to me about her experience of absorption, "It didn't begin with my marriage. It began in my childhood, especially in the way I learned to relate to my parents. I found it was safe to obey them, but in the process, I developed a core image of myself as a person incapable of making my own decisions. Instead of freely choosing to obey my parents, I was really learning to devalue myself and depend totally on them for my identity. When I married, I just transferred this dependency to my husband."

THE HIGH COST OF CHANGE

Though my colleague's experience differed from Lorraine's, some of the dynamics were similar. And if Lorraine attempts to change some of her unhealthy patterns of relating to Tom, she can expect to encounter tempestuous seas. Her desire to go back to college and her push for an expression of her unique identity separate from her husband are most definitely going to rock the marital boat. Changing long-established patterns of relating means there will be rough sailing ahead for both of them. Some marriages don't survive when one person wants to grow and the other resists, particularly when the relationship has not been adequately nurtured before the change occurs or when the commitment to the marriage is weak. Lorraine will have to brave the risks as she begins her journey.

One thing is certain: Tom and Lorraine's neat definitions of submission and authority will no longer work for them. When submission masks a woman's willingness (even desire) to be absorbed by her husband, it is not biblical submission, whether that absorption stems from her fear of personal responsibility, a childhood loss of personhood, or some other personal reason. God does not call a woman to become a nonperson in her marriage in the name of "submission." And a husband who boxes his wife in (verbally, emotionally, financially, or physically) to "keep her in line" has grossly misinterpreted God's intention regarding his authority.

In an article entitled "For Better, for Worse," which appeared recently in *The Banner*, a weekly denominational magazine, an anonymous pastor's wife told about her ordeal of living for several years with a husband who physically abused her. This unhappy woman described herself as having been a barometer wife (though she did not use that term) before seeking help through counseling. She wrote,

> I reasoned that I had married my husband "for better, for worse" and that society expected me to be submissive to and dependent on my husband. The thought of removing myself from this relationship brought with it a fear unlike any other I had ever known, because I had been taught, in one way or another, that without my husband I did not exist. My dependency on him, my fears, and my feelings of inferiority kept me in this abusive relationship. I felt trapped, used, unloved, lonely, confused, worthless, bitter, and angry.[1]

Do you perceive what had been going on beneath the surface of this marriage, hidden from everyone and only vaguely understood even by the woman herself? She allowed herself to become a "Christian nobody," willing to settle for mere crumbs in a relationship that should have provided a feast of affirmation and protection. That pastor's congregation never suspected he struggled with an anger so great that he abused the one he was most responsible for guarding and cherishing. Until his wife reached a point of desperation, both were living out a destructively unbiblical concept of submission in which she had lost her way because she had lost herself. When God in His wisdom designed marriage and honored it as a reflection of His love for His people, surely He never intended the relationship to look like this one.

JESUS' EXAMPLE

By way of contrast, consider how Jesus Christ related to people while He was here on earth. He was the perfect lover and never overpowered any person, male or female. He could have used His divine power to force His way, but instead He modeled that authority must be used to bless, not exploit. Even in confronting people with their sin (such as the incidents involving the Pharisees), Jesus treated them with dignity. He respected them enough to speak the truth forcefully but without manipulating. A man secure in His maleness, He did not boss men or women. He invited all to live up to their potential and to use their God-given gifts for the arrival and extension of His Kingdom.

In a culture accustomed to keeping women in "their place," Jesus gave women a new and wonderful place. For example, the Jewish model for education at that time provided for the local rabbi to teach little boys to read and write Hebrew so they could understand and obey God's instructions in the Holy Torah; however, little girls received no formal education. In *Man and Woman in Biblical Perspective*, Dr. James Hurley wrote regarding the teaching of Jewish women in Jesus' day, "Women were generally assumed by the rabbis to be persons incapable of learning about religious things." In fact, "some rabbis actually forbade instructing them in religious affairs."[2]

In sharp contrast to those rabbis, Jesus never discouraged women from using their minds; He encouraged them to listen to and learn from Him. Mary of Bethany sat at Jesus' feet, listening to Him teach, while her sister Martha busied herself in the kitchen preparing supper. When Martha complained that Mary's place was not to learn but to help her, Jesus insisted that Mary's choice was a good one (Luke 10:38-42). He seemed not to have been threatened by Mary's questions and desire for education. Rather, He affirmed her intellectual and spiritual inquisitiveness. According to Dr. Hurley,

The foundation-stone of Jesus' attitude toward women was his vision of them as *persons* to whom and for whom he had come.

He did not perceive them primarily in terms of their sex, age or marital status; he seems to have considered them in terms of their relation (or lack of one) to God. . . . Jesus, unlike the rabbis, taught women, willingly receiving them among his followers. They were persons for whom he had a message and were treated as such.[3]

Jesus also affirmed women's individual value and contributions by allowing several well-to-do Jewish women, some of them married, to follow Him and use their gifts (financial and otherwise) for serving Him. The Judaism of Jesus' time, in contrast to Old Testament practices, assigned separate places to Jewish men and women in the Temple and synagogues, presumably to keep the men from being tempted by the women during their times of worship.

Jesus, however, observed no such prohibition. He allowed women not only to learn from Him but also to travel with Him and His disciples. Dr. Hurley stated, "The presence of these women must have been a matter of considerable comment as Jesus traveled. It was not uncommon that a rabbi should have a band of followers; it was most unusual that the followers should include women."[4] Luke even lists some of their names: Mary Magdalene, Joanna the wife of Cuza (the manager of Herod's household), and Susanna (Luke 8:1-3). They undoubtedly made Jesus' mission financially possible. Luke said, "These women were helping to support [Jesus and His disciples] out of their own means" (Luke 8:3).

Jesus' relationship with them illustrates both His esteem for women and His glad willingness to have them develop and use their giftedness in meaningful ways to advance His Kingdom. It is hardly the picture of a man dominating or controlling women, though that was usually the case in Jewish society then.

Jesus never devalued women, not even outcast women. Rather, He taught that in God's economy women as well as men are worth His time, His touch, His esteem, and His gifts. Both are equally capable of seeking and finding God. In fact, Jesus honored a woman, Mary Magdalene, with His first appearance after His resurrection, entrusting to her and the other women (whose testimony would have been inadmissible in a Jewish court because they were female) the first triumphant news of His victory over death. If Jesus was that affirming of the gifts and value of women, how can we consider biblical a wife's loss of her identity to her husband in the name of submission?

DESTRUCTIVENESS OF MARITAL ABSORPTION

Furthermore, what makes us think it is good for husbands to have their wives refuse to develop their identities? Was Lorraine loving Tom or only herself when she refused to risk being herself? A woman cannot love her husband and simultaneously be consumed with fear for her emotional safety. Tom did not feel deeply loved by Lorraine; he sensed her fear and knew she was not responding to him freely and gladly.

A wife's fearful submission may make her husband feel powerful, but his desire to be genuinely trusted and spontaneously loved will not be satisfied. The women in Jesus' life fearlessly trusted Him because they sensed that His love for them was open and nonexploitive. In glad response they gave their love to Him and added a rich dimension to His life.

In an alive marriage relationship a wife receives her husband's love with joy, and in response she delights and challenges him with her unique gifts and personality. If, instead, she fears him and sacrifices her personhood by becoming absorbed in his, she will have nothing to give him. Thinking herself biblically submissive, she will actually be cheating him of her love and denying him one of life's greatest pleasures—the blending of two individuals, male and female, into one creative whole. Both lose out when one gets lost.

In *The Intimate Marriage,* R.C. Sproul related an interaction he had with his wife, Vesta, that illustrates this principle. When he expressed a desire to totally and completely know her soul, she responded with unexpected resistance, saying that she wanted to keep some part of herself that would be hers alone. R.C. recorded this about the ensuing discussion:

> As we talked it out, certain things became clear. She expressed her desire to be a genuine helpmate to me. She then explained her feeling about the crisis that role can produce—the loss of personal identity. She said she didn't want to be merely "Mrs. Sproul"; she wanted an identity of her own. She wisely reminded me that the biblical union of two people into one

flesh did not involve the annihilation of personal identity. . . .
I expressed the desire to know her soul in order to love it, but
she had gotten the impression that I wanted that knowledge in
order to possess her soul and exploit it. That's the fear, and the
danger is real. If I want that knowledge, I must labor to
establish that safety. Any other approach would be rape.[5]

Dr. James and Mrs. Shirley Dobson, whose Focus on the Family
radio ministry is committed to encouraging the betterment of marriage
and family life, were interviewed recently by the staff of *Today's
Christian Woman* magazine. They were asked to describe how they (and
especially she) handle the potentially divisive matter of his very strong
public identity and position. The interviewer questioned Dr. Dobson:
"How has Shirley been able to maintain her own identity in your
relationship?"

His answer reflects a far more balanced perspective on marriage
than is found in the relationship between a barometer woman and a
domineering man:

> When you have a husband whom God has blessed and who is
> well known for any reason, whether it is a ministry or a
> business, his wife often suffers from an identity problem.
> Shirley has been through that. She said to me when she was
> about thirty-five, "I know very clearly who you are, but I'm not
> positive who I am." It was an important day when Shirley and I
> realized that she needed something apart from what we had
> together. . . .
>
> My point is that it's difficult for either spouse when
> everything focuses on the partner. The other one finds himself
> or herself saying, "Isn't it wonderful how the Lord is blessing
> you? I'm glad that your talents are being used. But tell me once
> again, who am I, and where do I fit into God's plan?"

Then Shirley responded to her husband's comments by making
this follow-up observation: "I made the choice early in our marriage to
be Jim's team member. But I still needed to know what God wanted of
me as my children grew older. It took me several years to figure that
out."[6]

SUMMING UP

God's relationship with each of us as His children frees us to be individually what we're meant to be and to do all we're gifted by Him to do. Bondage is never His way, neither with men nor women. It often seems easier to become a slave to someone else's expectations than to risk living free and making mistakes and creating waves. Many women refuse to risk the pain and joy of discovering and being who they are as unique children of God.

Slavery, however noble it sounds when we call it self-denial or wifely submission, is not at all what God intends. Far too often emotional slavery is applauded in the Christian community when a wife sells out her identity to become a yes woman to her husband in the name of submission. A husband does not need a yes woman; he needs a companion willing to respect him enough to be her own person and tell him who she really is and what she really thinks. A wife should be able ⬅ to be in her husband's presence essentially who she is in his absence. Submission masking absorption makes God cry—for both partners. A woman's unique personhood is a terrible thing to waste.

NOTES:
1. "For Better, for Worse," *The Banner,* June 3, 1988, page 12.
2. James B. Hurley, *Man and Woman in Biblical Perspective* (Grand Rapids: Zondervan Publishing House, 1981), page 63.
3. Hurley, page 83.
4. Hurley, page 91.
5. R.C. Sproul, *The Intimate Marriage* (Wheaton, Ill.: Tyndale House Publishers, 1986), pages 24-25.
6. James and Shirley Dobson, *Today's Christian Woman,* May/June 1988, page 76.

QUESTIONS FOR THOUGHT AND DISCUSSION

1. Clarify the difference between caring about someone and being a caretaker by giving examples of persons with these behavior patterns.

2. Why do you think God is displeased when a woman loses her identity in her husband's?

3. In 1 Corinthians 11:3 Paul taught that "the head of the

woman is man." Explain how Tom's behavior is or is not in keeping with a husband's headship role in marriage.

4. What nonbiblical motivation might Lorraine have in her "submission" toward Tom?

5. Based on the way Jesus related to the Samaritan woman at the well (John 4:1-42), describe how He esteemed and valued women without domineering them.

C·H·A·P·T·E·R

3

PEACEFUL WATERS:
Submission as Appeasement

When Walter came through the door, Cindy knew immediately what the rest of the evening was going to be like. Hers had already been a difficult day of housecleaning in preparation for dinner guests, complicated by the children's arguing. To calm the troubled waters, Cindy had excused Denise from her piano practice and had promised Tommy a Saturday movie outing if he would shower and dress for dinner without further upsetting his sister. Then Walter arrived.

Cindy recognized his look. It said, "I've had a bad day. Don't cross me, or you and I will both be sorry." Not only was there going to be no help from Walter to prepare the house or the dinner for their guests, there was also going to be one more person for Cindy to please before company arrived if her little dinner party was to avoid being a social disaster. She greeted Walter with a smile (somewhat strained) and settled him in his recliner with the newspaper to "rest up for the Wilsons." Then she hurried to let the children know that Dad was tired and they should not fight or make too much noise for the next hour before supper. She went back to the kitchen to take care of final arrangements before the Wilsons' arrival.

Cindy's anxieties were far from over once the guests were seated at the table. In fact, her inner tension increased. The Wilsons were members of their church, and Cindy worried that Walter's prayer might not be quite right. She suggested to Walter that perhaps Jim Wilson would be willing to say grace before the meal. Walter asked, and Jim agreed.

That hurdle cleared, Cindy worked her way through dinner acutely conscious of how Walter was doing. She corrected him when he used the wrong verb tense and steered the conversation away from subjects about which she knew he could wax heated and even a little unreasonable. She did not ask Jim about his golf game (Walter was jealous of his scores), nor did she ask Alice about her promotion to supervisor (Walter disapproved of women "bossing men"). And there were the children to worry about. Cindy never knew when they might say something to embarrass or anger Walter, so she ran interference to avoid a mid-dinner "scene." All in all, it was not a relaxing meal for her.

Dinner through and dishes done, the Wilsons finally departed, and the children were sent to bed. Then came the follow-up tension. Cindy played the role of defending the Wilsons from Walter's negative opinions about their views, their clothes, their religious positions. When Cindy finally dropped into bed, she wondered why she was so very exhausted, and Walter wondered why he could not seem to interest her in a little "party" the way he usually could.

THE APPEASEMENT LIFESTYLE

Family peacekeepers, also known as den mothers to the world, are usually exhausted. It is no mean task keeping happy and unhassled the people who occupy their world, and someone has to foot the emotional bill. In *The Pleasers: Women Who Can't Say No—and the Men Who Control Them,* Dr. Kevin Leman says that appeasers "carefully navigate the oceans of life and make everything smooth for all on board. Peace at any price is often their motto, and they pay dearly."[1] Cindy had spent her day and most of her energy ensuring the success of her dinner party, seeing to it that everyone's needs—except her own—were met. When it was over, she felt good in spite of her exhaustion. Peacekeepers are inevitably fatigued if they feel good.

When appeasement like Cindy's happens in a Christian home, it is often considered godly submission. She looks like a wonderful wife, catering to Walter and making his home life as comfortable and hassle-free as possible. Her accommodating behavior is what someone might expect in a wife who desires to be a suitable helpmate for her husband. But does her style of submission qualify as biblical?

It depends on her motive. Why is Cindy really interested in keeping the peace? As she quiets the children, soothes Walter's irritation, and navigates the choppy waters of social interaction, what is there beneath her charming exterior that might suggest she is not merely interested in Walter's well-being? Why does she so often feel nervous and tight inside when they entertain instead of relaxing and enjoying their friends' company? What is really going on behind the masks in this relationship?

EVALUATING THE APPEASEMENT MARRIAGE

The public image of Walter and Cindy's marriage is generally quite positive. Jim and Alice Wilson, for example, like both of them. After the dinner party, they comment, "Walter is lucky to have a wife like Cindy. Think of the women we know from our jobs and in our church who would benefit from her example of submission!" To the Wilsons and the other members of their church, Walter and Cindy's marriage would rate about a B+.

How would Walter and Cindy evaluate the somewhat more realistic family level of their relationship? Walter likes Cindy's "submission." He says he has plenty of problems at work and doesn't need more when he comes home. It is fine with him that Cindy takes responsibility for their relationship; he considers that her strength. And Cindy hardly gives it a second thought; usually she is too busy calming some threatened turbulence. She loves Walter and wants to please him. Her culture has taught her that that is the woman's appropriate role, and she basically does not question it. The church they attend affirms what she is doing, and she relishes the approval.

Though Walter does not like the way Cindy seems to subtly tell him how to act, and though Cindy occasionally feels used and unappreciated, for the most part they are not complaining. They do not talk about her appeasing, but they think they have a pretty good marriage. On the family level, they would give their relationship about a B.

But what about the part of the marriage that remains hidden

behind the mask? Might there be reasons for Cindy's appeasement that have nothing to do with her genuine commitment to being a woman of God in her marriage relationship? Maybe she is invested in the goal of no-hassle in order to avoid her pain and fear of her husband's disapproval. The benefit she receives from protecting Walter from discomfort is that she shifts the balance of control in her direction. What is it that Cindy really wants? Is the power she has gained an adequate compensation for Walter's disregard of her and lack of tender involvement in her life?

What is happening within Walter? Is his relationship with Cindy deeply satisfying? Though he hates having his household boat rocked, sometimes her appeasing makes him feel a little managed, and that does not feel good. Her behavior undermines the very sense of strength he needs to risk the strong, involved leadership to which God has called him. If genuine love is to grow between these two, Walter must examine and change what it is he expects—even demands—from Cindy. And both must take an honest look behind her mask of submission.

APPEASEMENT AND ABUSE

Submission masking appeasement appears in various forms in marriages, but one particular extension of the appeasement mentality exists far too often in Christian marriages. Some wives who are committed to a policy of appeasement fall into the category of the abused. They are victims of emotional, verbal, physical, and even sexual abuse in their homes.

Abused women are appeasers to the extreme. For the sake of peace, these wives accept at their husbands' hands neglect, criticism, blame, and pain—both emotional and physical. They usually bury their pain in denial because they need to believe things are better than they really are. The appeasing abused woman clings to her submissive mask for fear of reopening old wounds or inviting new ones, so the abuse runs its predictably destructive course unabated. In its most devastating outgrowth, that of permitted incest, an appeasing wife will even sacrifice her daughter to the sexual abuse of her husband for the sake of not jeopardizing the marriage. Fortunately, not all abused women carry their appeasement this far.

One Woman's Abuse

I met a young woman recently who is struggling with how to deal with an abusive husband. His physical attacks on her and her children began some time ago and are becoming increasingly violent. She knew before she married him that he had a terrible temper, but she naively thought she would be able to change that once they were married. Unfortunately, it did not work out that way. Instead of decreasing, the abuse increased year after year despite her continual attempts to appease her husband.

About six months ago, she went to her pastor with her fear and concern. He quoted from 1 Peter 3: "Wives, in the same way be submissive to your husbands so that, if any of them do not believe the word, they may be won over without words by the behavior of their wives, when they see the purity and reverence of your lives." He told her that she was probably the only one in the world who could win her unsaved husband to the Lord, and she should submit to him as lovingly as possible.

Because this Christian wife wanted to obey the Lord and because she was not willing to deal with her unhealthy patterns of relating to her husband, she remained in the relationship without initiating any change. But the abuse has not stopped. Her husband has not dealt with his destructive habits, and she is worn down with the anxiety of trying to provide safety for herself and her children. Moreover, her guilt at not being able to "submit" is complicating an already difficult situation. She recently asked me in desperation, "What am I doing wrong? I want to be submissive, but I don't know how much more abuse I can take, especially with the children involved. What do you think I should do?"

Agonizing Consequences

What would you have said? Should she keep taking her husband's beatings? Is her pastor's explanation of submission biblical? Is she really loving her husband when she allows him to abuse her and the children and then to grovel for her forgiveness time after time? What can she do that would be loving toward her husband and at the same time be good for her and her children?

I have met countless Christian women like Cindy and this abused young wife, women caught in appeasement situations of many kinds.

Some have tried too hard to please the men in their lives, and in the process, they have lost the balance of asking that their need for love and esteem be met in return. Others are caught in more obviously abusive relationships, women related to alcoholics or drug addicts, battered women, victims or silent approvers of incest or other sexual abuse, or parishioners sexually abused by the very pastors to whom they turned for help. Many of these women were taught appeasement in the guise of Christian submission to authority, and the damage done—physically, emotionally, and especially spiritually—is incalculable.

Add to this the damage done to the children who emerge from those dysfunctional homes, and the problem is multiplied many times over. Not only do the children caught in abusive situations suffer, too, but they learn to imitate the dysfunction of their childhood families in their future family relationships. The growing participation of hundreds of thousands in organizations such as Adult Children of Alcoholics, for example, is strong evidence that a policy of appeasement in abusive families has profound and terrible long-term consequences. Appeasement is not a respectable option available to Christian women who do not want to upset the marital apple cart. Though often applauded as a virtuous attempt at submission, the appeasement mentality actually destroys families.

APPEASEMENT DYNAMICS

Most appeasers, especially those living in abusive relationships, fearfully hide their pain for years before becoming desperate enough to seek help. The abused pastor's wife described in the previous chapter kept her silence about her husband's violence out of fear of the consequences. As she said, "The abused are lonely, confused, terrified, and more than likely unable to contact a counselor because of the control the abuser has over them; often they fear the abuser will find out and become more abusive."[2]

Fear is at the heart of all relationships in which one partner stakes everything on appeasing the other in order to stay out of pain. I'm a recovering appeaser myself. For years I didn't even know I had any pain to hide because I was so enmeshed in others' lives. I wouldn't let myself feel angry because I thought it was unspiritual, and I would cry alone, if at all, about unkindnesses done to me. I worked hard to keep Bill safe from people's negative opinions, including my own. And I always apologized first, believing everything wrong had to be *my* fault. My behavior looked godly, but I wasn't in touch with what was really going on in my soul.

I didn't think I had any needs, and when I finally recognized that I did, I realized that what had powered my "self-denial" was fear, not love. It was not a fear regarding my physical well-being, but a deep fear for my personal inner safety that motivated my pacifying, particularly in my marriage. A wife may think that her interference-running helps her husband cope with life's everyday irritations (it's what I thought), but in fact she is more concerned with preventing the anger, pain, or rejection she will suffer if she admits her needs and refuses to simply keep the peace.

Essentially, she wants to stay safe. Children growing up in dysfunctional families, for example, learn that the unpredictable is dangerous and that the best antidote to unpredictability is crisis prevention, which translates into appeasing the abuser (or substance abuser) so that a crisis can be averted. The fact that it seldom works (the crisis usually happens anyway) is certainly no deterrent. The strategy is followed with something approaching fanatic commitment time and time again.

This fear of being emotionally battered or rejected or disappointed or harmed, which happens to all of us to one degree or another, carries over into adulthood, and the fear needs somehow to be managed. Doing whatever appeases the abuser in the short run seems reasonable, however discouraging the long-term results may be.

In homes where a spouse's "abuse" is much more covert than violent, the long-term consequences of the abuse-appeasement dynamic may be more difficult for the partners to identify. But the truth remains: When a woman's fear of personal pain is the motivator of submissive (i.e., appeasing) behavior, her submission is not biblical.

When Paul admonished Christian wives, in Ephesians 5:22, to "submit to your husbands as to the Lord," he did not have in mind for them to do what Cindy and my abused friend were doing. Appeasing and loving are not the same; they are opposites. Appeasement is rooted in fear and focuses on the protection of the appeaser, whereas love is rooted in courage and focuses on the need of the other. Love casts out fear, but fear cancels out love.

DAMAGE TO BOTH PARTNERS

Once again, we need to examine the underlying dynamics that operate when appeasement is a major factor in a marriage. There may be many complex reasons why a man uses his authority to keep his wife placating him and why his wife lets him. Though the appeasement lifestyle may appear to have its benefits, the effect of appeasement on a marriage relationship is always ultimately negative.

For one thing, a wife's appeasement damages her husband's image of himself as a man. Instead of having to draw from the Father's resources and then offer love and strength to his family, an appeased man is encouraged to be irresponsible because he never has to face the consequences of his wrong ways of dealing with his life (insensitivity to his wife and children, a demanding spirit, a violent temper, overdrinking, sexual perversion, or whatever). Because his wife protects him from her own or anyone else's honest feedback, he can avoid responsibility for his behavior and for shepherding his family in true biblical headship. It may feel good to him at the time, but she is really doing him a disservice. In fact, she is insulting him. By her appeasement, she is telling him that she does not think he can handle the stress of disruption so she will protect him from life's problems. How emasculating for a wife to buffer her husband (as she might her children) from the normal irritations and unexpected reversals that are part of every person's life!

The "managing" that Walter resented in Cindy flowed from his normal desire to be seen as adequate for the task of being husband and father in his home, though his resentment fought with his contentment at not having to face the hassles. Cindy's appeasing manipulation of Walter's world was not true biblical submission because it showed no deep respect for him.

I wasn't respecting Bill when I refused to admit I was angry about something he had done. Of course he knew anyway, and the underlying message of my silence was that he wasn't strong enough to handle my honest anger. What husband wants to be told, however subtly, that he is not the man his wife is?

A wife's appeasement is not good for her, either. My attempts to smooth out every wrinkle from the fabric of Bill's life forced me to control him and take responsibility for what he did—the very opposite of the glad responsiveness to his leadership we both deeply desired. A woman who plays the appeaser plays God, trying to work all things for everyone's good.

When submission and authority are in proper balance, the motive for a wife's submission is respect, not fear. An appeasing wife lives intimately with fear and operates toward her husband out of that fear, not out of respect and love. Her appeasement sabotages what she most longs for: a relationship with her husband in which she is secure in his strength and unafraid.

INNER CONTRADICTIONS

The underlying feelings between marriage partners caught in appeasement relationships are incredibly ambiguous. Often they genuinely love each other, yet their inner sentences about each other tell a completely different story. Bill and I were so in love when we married, yet we spent years hiding our true thoughts about each other. I never knew he resented my insistence that we attend church services twice on Sunday (he appeased me by going along and saying nothing), and he didn't realize I dreaded going sailing with him (I appeased him because of the fear of disappointing him). For years we thought we were doing the loving thing for each other. But love was not reigning in our hearts; resentment was.

Underneath the "patience" and "godly forbearance" of some appeasing wives is a seething cauldron of bitterness and fierce anger. Their external submission masks deep wells of discontent and desperate strategies of control and manipulation. And the unspoken thoughts of their husbands toward them are equally angry and resentful, because those "patient" women find countless ways to make their husbands pay for their faults. Often the men are deeply enraged, though they feel too guilty about their sin to confront the more subtle abuse of silent condemnation or long-suffering martyrdom inflicted on them by their quietly vindictive wives. It is a vicious emotional cycle, and in the years before the appeasement and/or abuse is finally dealt with honestly and openly, such a sundering of the relationship can occur in the spirit of a marriage that it is incredibly hard work to repair it even when help is finally sought. Manipulation through appeasement inevitably takes its toll.

JESUS AND APPEASEMENT

During Jesus' earthly pilgrimage, He was never an appeaser. He modeled genuine love, but without a need to keep the peace. Jesus was a peacemaker, winning eternal peace between God and man through the sacrificing of His very life. But He was not a peacekeeper, soft-pedaling or withholding truth in order to avoid conflict. He never looked for a fight, but He never ducked when He was confronted with one, either. When His enemies attacked Him, He neither ignored nor deflected their barbs. He met them head-on. In His hometown of Nazareth, for example, Jesus did not try to appease His fellow towns-men. Without flinching or backing down, He named their attitude of unbelief, even though it resulted in their attempted execution of Him (Luke 4:24-27).

Jesus handled the determined opposition of the Pharisees in similar fashion. When they merely *thought* critically about Jesus' possible Sabbath healing of the man with a withered hand (the perfect opportunity for an appeaser to avoid a confrontation), the Savior stood the misformed man before them all and openly challenged the incon-sistency in the Pharisees' Sabbath theology. Then He publicly restored the man's hand (Luke 6:6-11). Even when the Pharisees joined ranks with the turncoat Herodians to trap Jesus so they could have Him killed, Jesus did not back away. He answered them so straightforwardly and fearlessly that even the conspirators were amazed (Mark 12:13-17).

In the most obvious of Jesus' confrontations with His detractors, He locked horns with members of the entrenched religious establish-ment in Jerusalem, the real power structure behind the Judaism of His day. Seeing the sacred Temple violated by merchants and money-changers and turned into a lucrative marketplace for the Sanhedrin's benefit, Jesus overturned money tables, drove out vendors, and forcibly diverted traffic from the sacred place of prayer (Mark 11:15-17). His actions hardly suggest a philosophy of "peace at all costs"; He was uncompromising in defying His Father's enemies. Appeasement played no part in His approach to them.

What do we know about Jesus' relationships with the people to whom He ministered? Did He walk on eggshells with them? Hardly. He firmly confronted the rich young ruler with his materialism and challenged him to sell all he had. When the crowds wanted to crown Him (what a tempting time to play the appeaser!), He left the scene without so much as an explanation or an announced itinerary. Nor did He hesitate to call sin by its real name. The paralyzed man was forgiven his sin before he was healed—no pretense about the true nature of *his* problem. The woman caught in adultery was not "misguided"; she was told to go and sin no more.

Jesus refused to be a yes man even to those who loved Him; He called Peter "Satan" and openly rebuked James and John for their inexcusable ambition. While visiting in Bethany, Jesus frankly, though gently, told Martha that her sister Mary had chosen the better path. He refused to yield to His mother's pressure, and He chided Thomas for his unbelief. When Jesus interacted with His followers, friends, and family, His goal was never to keep the peace but to move toward them in honesty and strong love. Appeasement was definitely not His style.

SUMMING UP

Husbands and wives trapped in appeasement relationships for whatever reason will not find the deep joy God intended marriage to provide because they are failing to love as Jesus loved. A wife's goal of safety, achieved by her desperate attempt to be den mother to the world so that events fall into their "proper" place, prevents both her husband and herself from loving freely and responsibly. Appeasers close themselves off from the very ones with whom they most desire intimacy, and invariably both partners lose out. Finally, they find themselves in that most painful of places, mutually bound covenantally to the person who should be, but is not, God's vehicle for meeting the heart's deep needs. How sad! And how sadly common, even among Christians.

NOTES:
1. Kevin Leman, *The Pleasers: Women Who Can't Say No—and the Men Who Control Them* (Old Tappan, N.J.: Fleming H. Revell, 1987), page 23.
2. "For Better, for Worse," *The Banner,* June 3, 1988, page 12.

QUESTIONS FOR THOUGHT AND DISCUSSION

1. Explain the difference between being a peacekeeper and being a peacemaker.

2. List five sinful peacekeeping things Cindy did during the events described at the beginning of this chapter.

3. What effect does the appeasement of a woman like Cindy have on her husband?

4. In what way is Walter sinning in the relationship?

5. How do you think a Christian woman who is being physically or verbally battered by her husband should show her submission to him?

6. What can you say about the relationship between appeasement and control?

7. Based on your reading of John 8:31-47, show how Jesus was not an appeaser.

C·H·A·P·T·E·R

4

HIDDEN AGENDA:
Submission as Manipulation

In the previous two chapters we examined some of the dynamics operating beneath the masks worn by women who outwardly appear submissive in their marriages. The barometer wife, who allows herself to become absorbed in her husband, and the appeasing wife, who sacrifices everything for the sake of peace, are not showing their husbands true submission, regardless of how godly they seem on the outside. In fact, neither barometer-living nor peacekeeping ultimately benefits either partner in the marriage, because it is God's design that the relationship be built on mutual respect and reciprocal caring.

A third mask of submission that can be a deterrent to the growth of genuine love involves a wife's hidden agenda for her husband. She has a plan for him that she does not tell him about and may not have articulated even to herself. She may mouth submissive intentions and even carry in her heart a desire to be a biblically submissive wife, but because she is operating according to this hidden agenda, her actions will follow not Scripture but her deep longings to have her needs met by her husband. Neither spouse may be conscious of what is going on, but the husband in his spirit will be resistant to (and resentful of) his wife's strategies. Her "submission" masks manipulation.

A MANIPULATION MARRIAGE

Jane and Ted married young, only a year out of high school. They had dated off and on since junior high, and Ted was considered the catch of his class. Their courtship had been stormy, and Jane had broken off with him more than once when she found he had secretly dated other girls—once even after their engagement. Ted always insisted those other girls meant nothing to him, and Jane wanted to believe him, telling herself that after the wedding she would never have to be jealous again. Unconsciously, she began to cherish an ideal image of Ted she was certain she could help him achieve once he was committed to her by marriage vows.

Things went well at first. Jane was proud to be married to a man as good-looking and outgoing as Ted. They continued to be active in the church where they had grown up together, and their transition to married life was fairly smooth.

After the wedding, Ted completed his two-year associate degree in business while Jane worked. A year and a half later, their first child was born and their second a year after that. Their move to another state, when Ted finished school, was traumatic for Jane, exhilarating for Ted. Throughout those early years, Jane stayed too busy to be consciously aware that her goal of winning Ted's warm involvement in her life was unachieved. She would have told you she was happy if you had asked. But there were unexpected impulses of loneliness and fear that sometimes stabbed through her cheerful exterior. She never told anyone about them. She thought no one would understand; she herself did not understand.

Ted and Jane had been married less than five years when he was forced by circumstances to confess to her an affair that had been ongoing for three months. Jane was devastated, though she had suspected his infidelity for some time. She wondered if this was his first illicit liaison, but did not dare ask. Together they visited their minister, but he was reluctant to get involved because Jane was so emotional. Together they sought counseling elsewhere. Ted never expressed sorrow for being unfaithful, but he did display an interest in continuing the marriage. For a while he became more attentive to Jane, but she never resolved her anger or sense of betrayal. She knew, however, that she could not manage being a parent to their two small children without Ted, so she learned to ignore her true feelings and tried to make herself forgive him, as the minister and the counselor had encouraged her to do.

In the years that followed, Jane continued to pursue her unspoken goal of changing Ted into the caring, thoughtful man she felt she needed to feel good about herself. She tried everything she could to earn Ted's love and esteem. She devoted herself to her house and children and redoubled her efforts to become a kind and submissive Christian wife in order to keep Ted interested in and faithful to her. She obeyed what he told her to do and seldom complained. She always supported Ted in public, and even when they were alone, she tried not to cross him because she knew how he could put her down with a look or a comment.

Her conscious goal in her marriage was to please Ted, forgive him for his wandering eye, and make his home life as attractive as possible. But her underlying goal was to get him to be more thoughtful of her. Her efforts were largely unconscious; she did not think she was trying to manage Ted's life. Their friends at the church to which they had transferred after the affair considered Jane a good example of biblical submission.

Ted, for his part, continued to be a diligent and successful breadwinner, enjoying both the challenge and the independence of owning a business. He remained active in the local church, eventually achieving a leadership role in the congregation. Discussing various aspects of theology with the pastor was one of his most satisfying pastimes. He was content to have Jane as his wife and the mother of his children; he trusted her to do an excellent job of managing the house and family.

But Ted was committed to resisting the pressure of Jane's emotional clawing. Thus, in addition to his interactions with their mutual friends from church and the neighborhood, Ted developed a social life of his own from which Jane was largely excluded—men and women associated with his business with whom he would sometimes spend one or two nights a week. He didn't exactly lie to Jane about these events, but neither did he offer any unsolicited information about what happened. He took a certain pleasure in Jane's jealousy, though he always did his best to make her feel guilty and foolish for not trusting him.

As Jane became more committed to her goal of changing Ted, their relationship continued to deteriorate. Jane tried to manage the way Ted "came across" to people, especially their church friends. When they went out socially, she would sometimes correct the details of his anecdotes, and she laughed at his jokes even when they weren't funny. Sometimes he said biting things (he could be cruel when he wasn't being charming), and she would try to ease the tension by making a funny remark or changing the subject. Once, when he got angry with the pastor and refused to attend church for several weeks, she told their friends that he had been out of town a lot that month. Jane was deeply invested in having Ted look good.

Yet Jane also felt she could not trust Ted after the affair, and when he was late for dinner, she would ask him (offhandedly, she thought) subtle questions about where he'd been and with whom. Sometimes she would call the office to ask him a question that didn't really need an answer right then. She checked his clothes and occasionally his mail, and once she even came home early from a women's Bible study meeting to be sure he was home alone with the children. Jane felt an urgent need to know about and control Ted's life both with her and away from her. It had become a compulsion.

One day not long ago, Jane invited me to have lunch with her. As we chatted over coffee and dessert, she seemed to be gathering her courage for something. Finally, she confided with a catch in her voice, "I think Ted is involved in another affair."

She went on to tell me the details that supported her suspicions, then added with more than a touch of anger, even vengeance, "I've asked my neighbors and one of my friends at church to do some spying on Ted. He'll never suspect it. This time I'm going to catch him and make him pay for what he's been doing to me!" Everything hung on what her "detective" friends would discover about Ted. When their report came in, she would decide what to do.

EVALUATING THIS MARRIAGE

Looking at the three tiers of this marriage, what do we find? The public opinion of the relationship was mixed, depending on which group was doing the observing. Ted's business associates knew his marriage was empty at best; they would have rated it in the D range. At church the facade was more carefully preserved. Ted never complained, and Jane never told anyone how she really felt, so no one suspected how bad things were. Most church members found Ted an energetic worker and a generous giver, though possibly somewhat too aggressive. They considered Jane submissive and Ted a leader; they would have given the couple a strong B.

On the family level of this relationship, both Ted and Jane knew they were having problems. Jane, having worked so futilely to make things better (according to her definition of *better*), was more in touch than Ted was with the uncertainty of their future relationship. Both wanted the marriage to work, but for altogether different reasons. They knew they were drifting apart. They would have given themselves about a C-.

But things were much worse than that on the inside level of the relationship. Jane and Ted were alienated from, even hostile toward, each other in the secret personal places they seldom examined. The sentences they unconsciously spoke to themselves about each other were angry and destructive. Jane deeply resented Ted's infidelity and his subsequent secrecy and distancing of himself from her. She did not feel loved, and she blamed him for it. Her desire for revenge was escalating in spite of herself, and she did not know how to stop it. Her frustration at her inability to change Ted had brought her to the edge of hatred, yet she could not free herself from her desperate dependence on him.

Ted hated having to live under Jane's manipulation and continual surveillance. He disrespected her because of her constant clinging, and he backed away from involvement in her life because the emotional price was more than he was willing to pay. He needed marital "success" in the eyes of his business associates and church friends, and he certainly desired intimacy in his marriage. But he wanted those things without taking any responsibility. He wanted Jane to be there for him without his taking any risks at which he might fail. Although her fearful submission to his demands made him feel good, her corresponding manipulation angered him because he knew she also deeply disrespected him. He manipulated her by his secrecy and disinterest, and Jane could not understand why she felt trapped. Neither spouse knew how to settle the impasse. On the inner level of this marriage, it was failing altogether.

ABSENCE OF SPIRITUAL LEADERSHIP

As I pondered my conversation with Jane, I recalled a conversation with another friend several months earlier. This Christian friend was married to a man who was good to her but was interested only in the surface activities of the Christian life. She believed God had designated the husband as spiritual head of the family, and she was more than willing to be a submissive wife. But her husband was content to keep his church involvement casual and his spiritual life to himself. He was a good husband and father, and he went to church to please his wife. However, that was as far as he wanted it to go.

My friend refused to sacrifice her goal of making her husband into a spiritual leader. Her concern is shared by countless Christian wives who are tired of always saying the mealtime prayer and taking the children to church or Sunday school without their fathers and making Christmas more than mere gift-getting. They know that taking over the husband's spiritual leadership will result in an upside-down marriage relationship, but they also know they cannot disregard their children's spiritual lives. They worry about the message their children receive from their fathers' unconcern. Some are married to men who are unabashedly unbelievers. Many more are married to men who say they are Christians but abdicate their spiritual responsibility. These wives are caught between a willingness to submit (to a nonexistent authority) and a compulsion to take over to prevent spiritual chaos in the home. It is not an easy place to be, and a discouragingly high percentage of Christian wives live with this frustration.

HIDDEN "SPIRITUAL" AGENDA

When caught on the horns of this dilemma, many a Christian wife will adopt a hidden agenda for her husband's spiritual life. She will work, often unconsciously, toward getting him to measure up to her internal image of what a spiritual leader ought to be like. She may urge him to attend church or Sunday school, thinking that if he comes under the teaching of a godly man, he might get the idea and decide to become one himself. Or she may suggest ways for her husband to handle family devotions—whether he wants to or not—but take over if he does not follow through.

The possibilities are endless for spiritually force-feeding husbands. I had a secret spiritual agenda for Bill, and I blush to remember how I managed to coerce him into teaming up with me as leaders of a youth group in a church we once attended. I thought he would grow in grace if I could make him responsible for nurturing those young people. My maneuverings not only violated Bill's freedom of choice, but also squelched his spirit and damaged our relationship, all in one fell swoop. (And I thought I was a wonderfully submissive wife!)

If the direct approach fails, a Christian wife married to a spiritually uninvolved husband might conveniently arrange to be listening to a Christian television or radio program when he arrives home from work. He might find brochures for men's weekend retreats or Christian marriage enrichment seminars next to his favorite chair. Or she might manipulate social engagements with Christian couples, hoping the husbands will be role models for her husband.

After years of exercising unsuccessful strategies for programing Bill's spiritual life, I finally confronted him one day with my spiritual loneliness and my need to have him involved with me. I tearfully begged him to join me in my walk with the Lord, but he refused in no uncertain terms. He said he was tired of my pressuring him to be something he was not and did not want to be. I was crushed and decided I would have to pursue my Christian pilgrimage without him, lonely though that might be. It was years before I could recognize the blessing in Bill's refusal to submit to my spiritual manipulation. He needed to make his own decisions about his relationship with the Father, just as I did. One Holy Spirit is enough for anyone.

DYNAMICS OF MANIPULATION

When a woman experiences the pain of disappointment because of her husband's flaws—whether physical, social, moral, or spiritual—she invariably looks for a way to ease that pain. Her most common tactic is to try to change her husband into the kind of man she thinks she needs and believes God intended for her to have. The absence of a wife's genuine acceptance of her husband (and he feels it keenly) sabotages his confidence in himself and in her. The unspoken rejection implied by her manipulation, however well-intentioned, undermines the very environment of trust and openness she needs if she is to flourish as a loved woman. It is ironic that often a Christian woman's desire to be submissive to a godly man is at the heart of her manipulation, which is the opposite of and counterproductive to the submission she desires.

In an even more ironic twist, sometimes the way a Christian woman practices being "submissive" is itself manipulative. I have known women to incorporate submissive behaviors into their marital styles of relating because they see that as the key to pleasing and thus changing their husbands. It is right for a woman to want to please her husband, but she must honestly face her motives if she is to love him as God intends. Some marriage books teach submission as biblical without dealing with motivation, which is what ultimately determines whether or not that submission is truly godly. And some Christian women who read those books follow the suggestions regarding submissive behavior only as a way to manipulate their husbands so they can get what they want.

However, a man knows when he is being taken in. His wife's submissive behavior, if it has a price tag on it, will eventually break down, and it will cost her his respect. It is true that God's principle regarding a wife's submission to her husband's authority works. But "work" should not be taken to mean "work to get what you want" or "work to get your husband to change" or even "work to save your marriage." Sometimes what a woman wants may be a very godly goal— having her husband saved or having him take a more active role in the spiritual life of the family, for example. Nevertheless, submissive behavior motivated by a wife's ulterior motive of changing her husband is not biblical submission. Such "submission" violates another principle taught and modeled by Jesus, the principle of loving freely with *agape* love, no strings attached.

JESUS' *AGAPE* LOVE

When Jesus related to the people in His life, He never tried to manipulate them. Though He unerringly knew and said what was best for everyone, He never forced anyone, overtly or covertly, to do what He knew was best. He always left individuals free to decide for themselves.

Perhaps the most notable example of Jesus' openhanded loving is seen in His experience with a rich young ruler who came to Him one day seeking the way to eternal life (Mark 10:17-22). Jesus told him the way to life was to obey perfectly the commandments, and the ruler replied that he had always done so. Mark recorded that "Jesus looked at him and loved him" (verse 21), then told him to sell everything he had and contribute the proceeds to the synagogue benevolent fund. Jesus loved that young man with a perfect love, and He also told him exactly how to change so that he could live the abundant life he was seeking. The Lord of the universe offered perfect love and perfect wisdom.

But He applied no pressure. Jesus allowed that man He loved to choose for himself, and then He let him walk away from what would have made his life complete. If I had been there, I think I would have run after that young man and grabbed his cloak and said, "Didn't you hear what Jesus said? That's good advice, young man! You ought to take it if you know what's good for you!" If he had still walked away, I might have kept a lookout for him so I could mention it to him again. Or maybe I would have written him a note reminding him of Jesus' love and wisdom and repeating Jesus' advice so he would be sure to do what was "good for him."

But that was never Jesus' way with anyone. Central to His loving was His letting go. Jesus recognized and honored an integral part of every person's humanity since Adam: the freedom to choose good or evil for oneself. From the beginning of God's dealing with mankind, He has refused to treat anyone as a puppet within His power. Instead He allows persons the right of choice. God balances choice with consequences (and certainly He draws irresistibly through His Spirit those He has chosen), but He never withdraws the right to choose from men or women.

Unfortunately, we seldom relate to each other with that same lack of manipulation. Lacking the conscious vital union to His Father that made Jesus' life purposeful and complete, we too often seek our wholeness through attempting to control others. Focusing on what we think others should be (for our benefit), we miss becoming the open channels of God's love we're designed to be in this world.

SUMMING UP

Submission is often a mask women hide behind as they pursue their real goal of manipulating their husbands. The charade in which Jane found herself was that of acting a submissive role while exercising manipulative strategies for getting what she thought she needed from her husband. In a way, though her pain was real and her prayers for relief heartrending, it was really a blessing from God that her manipulation was not working. It would not have been good for her or for Ted if her strategies had been successful. Though her needs were legitimate, whatever good feelings she might have enjoyed if Ted had capitulated to her demands would have been corroded by his resentment. In fact, even her unsuccessful manipulation was already having that effect. More important, if Jane had succeeded in manipulating Ted, she would never have had the opportunity to examine her sinful motives and to learn to love Ted as God intended. In short, God had more in mind for Jane than to reward her unloving attempts to control her husband.

And Ted needed to examine what was behind his mask of authority as well. The strategies of retreat and control he was hiding behind in his marriage were far from the no-strings-attached love husbands are called to offer to their wives. His pain was as real as Jane's, and his hidden agenda of manipulating her while staying free of her manipulation was as sinful as Jane's goal of changing him. The failure of his mask of authority to bring him inner satisfaction was God's gift to him, forcing him to recognize the marital games both spouses were playing. Other-managing was as much his problem as it was hers.

Manipulation masquerading as submission or as authority falls short of God's intention for the marriage relationship, as does submission masking absorption and appeasement. But that leaves us with some significant unanswered questions. What, then, is biblical submission? What is a godly exercise of authority? Can submission and authority be defined by their external evidences? How do they operate at the deep inner levels of a relationship? Is it even possible for a fallen wife to be biblically submissive to her fallen husband in a fallen world? Can a fallen husband genuinely lead a fallen wife according to the biblical model?

To find answers, we must discover what Scripture says husbands and wives legitimately need in marriage. Then we must examine the impact of the Fall on that most intimate of bonds, and the way sinful self-protection operates to destroy the oneness God designed for marriage. Finally, we must look at our need for repentance as prerequisite to true submission to God and to each other in marriage. Part 2 will deal with these topics.

QUESTIONS FOR THOUGHT AND DISCUSSION

1. Explain how both Jane and Ted are lonely in their marriage.

2. Think of a marriage you know well, perhaps your parents' or your own. What do you think the hidden agenda of each partner might be?

3. Why should I be grateful that my manipulation to get Bill to join me on my spiritual pilgrimage didn't work?

4. Read the account of Jesus' encounter with Nicodemus (John 3:1-21) and list at least three ways Jesus *could have* but *did not* manipulate Nicodemus to think or act in a particular way.

5. Briefly tell how the Old Testament women listed below tried to control the people or circumstances of their lives. Include the results of their manipulation.

•Sarah (Genesis 16)
•Rebekah (Genesis 25:19-28, Genesis 27)
•Jezebel (1 Kings 16:30-31, 18:4, 19:2, 21:1-16; 2 Kings 9:30-37)

2

KNOWLEDGE:
Understanding the Masks

5

GOD'S MARRIAGE DESIGN:
Reflecting His Image

In the first section of this book, we examined the ways in which many Christian men and women who embrace authority and submission as biblical have tried to live out those commitments in their marriages, but underneath the surface of their lives several crucial issues are left unexplored. Often the authority and the submission they are practicing are not working to make them more spiritually alive or their marriages happier, and many are getting discouraged. A superficial understanding of submission that ignores not only the legitimate needs of men and women but also their innate bentness to self-sufficiency leaves many Christians frustrated in their marriages and convinced that God just did not know what He was asking when He had Paul and Peter write about submission. Certainly, they reason, God did not have *their* husbands or *their* wives in mind when He handed down His instructions for Christian marriage.

But the testimony of Scripture is that God is a loving God who intends good for His people (male and female). Jeremiah records that the Lord declared, "For I know the plans I have for you . . . plans to prosper you and not to harm you, plans to give you hope and a future" (Jeremiah 29:11). Obedience to God's commands for us always moves us toward that hope and future, however difficult those commands are to obey. Paul insists that God's "commandment is holy, righteous and good" (Romans 7:12). Therefore, we must conclude that what God asks of us in our marriages is not only good because He is good, but it is also good for us.

Assuming, then, that God's requirements of husbands and wives are good for us, we should explore what Scripture says about the fundamental nature of the relationship between men and women. To discover God's design for that relationship in marriage, we must begin at Creation, before the Fall.

GOD'S DESIGN

From the beginning, God intended marriage—the joining of one male and one female in intimate union with each other. God could have established any order for society that He wanted, and what He chose was to reflect His nature by creating both man and woman, bringing them together in the institution of marriage. Genesis 1:27 tells us that on the sixth day "God created man in his own image, in the image of God he created him; male and female he created them."

What does it mean to be created in God's image? Books have been written and entire theologies built around the topic, but we will examine only three truths suggested by this verse: the equality of male and female, their capacity for intimacy, and the initiator-responder roles of husband and wife.

Designed for Equality

First, note that both male and female were equally created in God's image. There is no suggestion in Scripture of superiority or inequality; both bore (and continue to bear) the stamp of God's image on their personhood, even though one was a male person and the other a female person. The biblical teaching about a wife's submission to her husband in no way connotes that she is inferior to him or that he is superior to her. The insinuation of female inferiority often correlated with submission is probably the most compelling reason many Christian women resent and resist the entire concept.

Part of the problem, of course, is that though female inferiority is not biblical, it is nevertheless deeply entrenched in the attitudes and practices of countless men and women today. Many men believe it because they have been conditioned to think it true, and they like the advantage it gives them. Many women believe it because of an inadequate affirmation of their unique value in childhood, adolescence, and/or adult womanhood. A woman whose worth and/or femaleness was unaffirmed (or worse yet, was abused) has internalized a negative image of herself as a woman, whether the damage came from her father directly, from a patriarchal society indirectly, or even from her mother as a sense of inadequate femaleness was modeled and passed down. Often instead of being changed and healed in later life, especially by her husband (as every damaged woman hopes), this negative self-image is reinforced by his invalidation of her feelings or opinions, by his criticism of or unfaithfulness toward her, or by his concerted efforts to keep her "in her place." When a man in a power position over a woman negates her value, he perpetuates the notion of female inferiority.

Unfortunately, this perverted exercise of male power (in contrast to loving leadership) occurs with discouraging frequency, even within the Christian Church and within Christian families. The result has been the sexual and emotional exploitation of countless Christian women, single and married, and it accounts for the loss of enormous giftedness and service for the Kingdom by God's female image-bearers. Christian wives often react to the submission principle in marriage precisely because that principle has been so often abused for the personal benefit or comfort of men who are invested in considering women inferior. But the equality of women with men, in terms of value to God and giftedness by Him, is clearly taught in Scripture, particularly in the Creation story. Both Adam and Eve were created to reflect the image of God, individually and in their union.

Designed for Intimacy

Second, being created in God's image means that Adam and Eve were designed to live the way God lives, in relationship with other personal beings. The Lord God said, "It is not good for the man to be alone. I will make a helper suitable for him" (Genesis 2:18). An important part of being God's image-bearers is that we have the capacity for intimate relationships, to know and to become known to God and to other human beings (especially, but not exclusively, in marriage). Adam and Eve were created with a need for each other, a need that was good and a need that each was designed to fill for the other. This desire for intimacy—not mere sexual intimacy but a meshing of soul and spirit as well—is both natural and good. God made us this way to reflect His nature, and we need not apologize for it.

In some wonderfully mysterious way, the relational nature of human beings created in God's image reflects the relational nature of God Himself as Trinity, Three Persons in One. God is a "social" Being, so to speak, and we human beings, whether single or married, image Him in our relational capacity and expectation.

God cannot be said to have needs within the Trinity in the sense that all created beings are dependent, needing something outside themselves to sustain them. Yet there is an otherness-in-unity within the Godhead, a mutual capacity and reciprocity of relationship within the Trinity, that is an integral part of who God is. Dr. Cornelius Plantinga, a professor of systematic theology at Calvin Theological Seminary, describes the Trinity as "a society overflowing with a zestful life of light, joy, mutuality and verve."[1] God Himself is more than One.

Yet intimacy is possible without loss of self. Within that "society" of Trinitarian oneness there is a distinctive otherness about the three Persons of God. Dr. Plantinga connects our understanding of the Trinity to our experience of oneness in the marriage relationship. He writes,

> [The] precincts of heaven are occupied by more than one divine person. Christian monotheism must include more than one divine thinker, doer, actor, lover. For if God the Father and the Son of God are "one," they are not one person. Their unity is more like a marriage in which two persons become one flesh, or like persons bound together in a single community.[2]

Thus, being created in God's image means, among many things, that human beings were designed to enjoy oneness in the community of believers and especially in the marriage relationship, but without negating the wonderful individuality of each person. Jesus prayed for His disciples and for all future believers, "Holy Father, protect them by the power of your name . . . so that they may be one as we are one" (John 17:11).

Husbands and wives were created to need and mutually complement (complete) each other, but not to lose their separateness or to give up their unique identity in their marriage—or in any relationship. When God brought Eve to Adam, Adam exclaimed joyously, "This is now bone of my bones and flesh of my flesh" (Genesis 2:23); but he experienced no confusion about the fact that she was marvelously, wonderfully *other*. The beauty of God's design was that He created each of them to fit together in mysterious oneness with the other—mentally, spiritually, emotionally, and physically—yet without losing their individuality.

Designed for Initiator-Responder Roles

A third aspect of being image-bearers of God is that Adam and Eve, though equal, were created with differing roles in their relationship, reflecting the unique functioning of Father, Son, and Holy Spirit within the Trinity. For example, to accomplish mankind's salvation, the Father sent the Son (John 3:16), who gladly obeyed His Father's will in everything (John 4:34) and whose work on Calvary was applied through the agency of the Holy Spirit in the hearts of men (Titus 3:4-7).

Scripture in no way implies the Son's inferiority by His submission to the Father, but clearly portrays the Father as "initiator" or head (1 Corinthians 11:3) and the Son as "responder" or the one who submits (1 Corinthians 15:24-28). It is a functional distinction within the Trinity, but it is not an inequality issue. The footnote to the 1 Corinthians 15 passage in the *NIV Study Bible* says, regarding Jesus' subjecting of all things to the Father,

> The Son will be made subject to the Father in the sense that administratively, after he subjects all things to his power, he will then turn it all over to God the Father, the administrative head. This is not to suggest that the Son is in any way inferior to the Father. All three persons of the Trinity are equal in deity and in dignity. The subordination referred to is one of function.[3]

The husband-wife relationship in Eden before the Fall reflected that initiator-responder aspect of God's Trinitarian image in mankind. Adam's need for human fellowship, which God acknowledged as legitimate ("It is not good for the man to be alone" [Genesis 2:18]), was wonderfully met by God's creation of Eve ("I will make a helper suitable for him" [Genesis 2:18]). Eve was created for Adam (1 Corinthians 11:8-9) to respond to his initiation (as his helper), as Adam was designed to meet Eve's need for strength and love. They needed each other (1 Corinthians 11:11-12) and meshed together perfectly. Together they received God's mandates: "Be fruitful and increase in number; fill the earth and subdue it. Rule over the fish of the sea and the birds of the air and over every living creature that moves on the ground" (Genesis 1:28). In their mutual and glad obedience to that mandate, Adam was leader and Eve his helper, and both found pleasure and satisfaction in the arrangement because it was how they were created to be.

Thus, it was no surprise that when God came to them after their disobedience, He called out to Adam as the one responsible (Genesis 3:9)—though both had eaten the forbidden fruit, both were hiding, and both received judgment for their sin. God asked for an explanation from Adam first, not Eve, because he stood as direction-giver in the relationship. Adam was responsible to answer for what had happened to elicit their mutual shame. Paul, who surely knew that Eve had sinned before Adam, nevertheless named Adam as the one through whom sin entered the world, in contrast to the One through whom salvation has come (Romans 5:12-13).

And though God pronounced judgment on both Adam and Eve because both had sinned, even the difference in their punishment (which we will examine in more detail in the next chapter) reflects the distinction present in their pre-Fall relationship. Adam's and Eve's roles as initiator and responder give evidence that they are God's image-bearers because the roles reflect differing functions within the Trinity.

These three facts about Adam and Eve as God's image-bearers (i.e., their equality, their capacity for intimacy with God and each other, and their differing roles within their relationship) are foundational to understanding the dynamics of what marriage was like before the Fall. In that first perfect match, husband and wife naturally considered and treated each other with the dignity and appreciation befitting equals. They neither begrudged nor despised the differences between the sexes; rather, they reveled in those differences and celebrated them for themselves and for each other. They also gloried in their intimacy, drinking deeply at the satisfying fountain of fellowship with God and oneness with each other. They enjoyed with no regret the satisfaction of being fully what God had designed them to be—Adam, the strong initiator, and Eve, the glad responder, as they carried out God's mandate to manage and protect the world He had created.

DIVINE AND HUMAN FELLOWSHIP

Before the Fall, Adam and Eve's intimacy with God in the garden must have been wonderful. Having been made by and for God, they instinctively recognized there was within them a need (unlike their need for each other) that by God's design could not be met by any human being. They knew that even in their rich enjoyment of each other, they were not "enough" for each other. What Pascal called the "God-shaped vacuum" in each of them was a place only God could fill because He had made it for Himself alone. Adam and Eve knew this without being told, and they unhesitatingly turned to God in their garden walks for the deep intimacy and fellowship with Him that neither of them was designed to provide for the other.

But what they could provide for each other they provided lavishly and without reserve. As Dr. Larry Crabb says in his book *Inside Out,* "[God's] plan really is quite simple. Adam and Eve were to turn to God as the strong one on whom they could depend and *then* to each other to both enjoy what the other uniquely provided and to give of themselves to enhance the other's pleasure."[4] Before the Fall, Adam and Eve enjoyed a perfect blend of personal fulfillment and oneness.

PERSONAL FULFILLMENT

We have few details regarding how Adam and Eve interacted before the Fall. But we know Adam affirmed the wonder and joy of God's gracious provision of a woman to receive and surround his gift of loving strength (Genesis 2:23). And surely Eve fulfilled God's intention for her to be a competent and willing helper for the man who offered himself to her as he initiated their mutual tasks (Genesis 2:18). Adam's authority before the Fall was never abusive or patronizing, nor was Eve's submission ever grudging or resentful. In mutual respect and cooperation they experienced the affirmation and adequacy to do the job God had called and equipped them to do.

Unaccustomed as we are to experiencing undiluted satisfaction in being strong (as husbands) and responsive (as wives) in marriage, we wonder what it must have been like for Adam and Eve to have lived married with absolutely no masks. They must have enjoyed an exquisite balance in all that they did, together or alone. Adam was no tyrant, imperiously ordering Eve to carry out his orders regarding her responsibility in Eden. Rather, he was a confident, strong, yet gentle leader providing oversight for accomplishing God's mandate. And Eve was no intellectual pygmy dwarfed by a giant Adam. She was an intelligent, sensitive, passionate, alive woman, regal and shameless in her nakedness and every bit an equal of Adam without besting him or flaunting her abilities. How he must have loved her, bone of his bones and flesh of his flesh, cohort of mind and spirit and body!

PERFECT ONENESS

Along with and blended throughout Adam and Eve's wonderful partnership was their oneness, their unobstructed communication of thought and heart. They were not shamed by their mutual need for intimate relationship. They turned to each other without apology to find that mutual need richly satisfied. They knew the unspeakable joy of being both openly known and unconditionally loved by another human being. In Eden before the Fall, mankind's innate longing for *agape* love was perfectly met for both husband and wife.

The delights of Eden will always remain for us a matter of conjecture. We may imagine, for example, how Adam and Eve talked late into the night, speculating about their world and each other, each offering the particular perspective—equal but different—that was God's gift. Together they had a clearer picture than either could have achieved alone. We covet for ourselves the satisfaction they must have experienced before the serpent introduced competition and bitterness into their workplace and playground and worship garden. And what was their "one flesh" passion like, unencumbered by inhibition or guilt, manipulation or exploitation? We cannot possibly understand what it would mean to be naked—emotionally and personally as well as physically—and to feel no shame about who we are because we would be totally accepted and acceptable. Life in Eden must have been wonderful.

GOD'S DESIGN DAMAGED

Unfortunately, we will never experience in this life God's perfect intention for marriage, that perfect blending of partnership and oneness, adequacy and security. The fall of Adam and Eve described in Genesis 3 marked the entrance of sin into God's design and unbalanced the relationship in every marriage union since then. After the Fall, Eden was irretrievably lost, and only in glimpses and fragments would any marriage afterward ever know it again this side of Heaven. Marriage as God intended it has never been the same.

However, some things did not change. Marriage itself remained. Adam and Eve did not stop being husband and wife. There was still a union, though an imperfect one. And God's blueprint for marriage remained as well: "For this reason a man will leave his father and mother and be united to his wife, and they will become one flesh" (Genesis 2:24). Though every marriage since Eden has been tainted to some degree by the husband's abdication or misuse of his authority and the wife's manipulation or refusal to submit to that authority, marriage between one man and one woman for life continues to be God's foundation for the social structure of His world. Moreover, though twisted by sin, their roles as initiator and responder remain God's loving model for His male and female image-bearers.

Marriage remains, according to God's design, not the only but certainly a primary relationship through which God's own love and encouragement for His children can flow. We are to be, as husbands and wives, the pipelines through which God pours His care and esteem into each other's lives. Each marriage partner can individually draw from God's unconditional love and enabling power, and then each can give to the other what he or she needs to experience acceptance and adequacy. Even in a fallen world, that is how it could and should work. In fact, marriage ought to be God's showcase to the world of His loving relationship with His people, based on the mutual but differing needs of husbands and wives.

GOD'S DESIGN REDEEMED

This is particularly true when we consider that God has redeemed His people through the atoning death and resurrection of Jesus, the Son of

God. Through Christ's finished work, it is possible for mankind to experience restored fellowship with God and the filling of the Holy Spirit, God's enabling agent for righteous living. Thus, believers can live redeemed lives, even (maybe especially) in their marriages. Though their sin nature repeatedly sabotages their resolve toward oneness, Christian spouses can and should make consistently redeemed choices to mutually esteem and more unconditionally love each other. In other words, they have the power to make pre-Fall choices, the kind of choices Adam and Eve made before the Fall in fulfilling their roles and selflessly loving each other. If marriage partners will rely on God to meet their deepest needs for acceptance and forgiveness, they can, in His strength, be more and more to each other the strong leaders and glad responders each needs the other to be.

But before we describe how fallen spouses are instructed by Paul to more consistently make pre-Fall choices, we must examine the effect of the Fall on Adam and Eve's relationship—and on every marriage since then. The next chapter will deal with that topic.

NOTES:
1. Cornelius Plantinga, "The Perfect Family," *Christianity Today,* March 4, 1988, page 24.
2. Plantinga, page 26.
3. *The NIV Study Bible,* Kenneth Barker ed. (Grand Rapids: Zondervan Bible Publishers, 1985), pages 1756-1757.
4. Larry Crabb, *Inside Out* (Colorado Springs, Colo.: NavPress, 1988), page 70.

QUESTIONS FOR THOUGHT AND DISCUSSION

1. Why do you think God emphasizes twice (Genesis 2:24 and Matthew 19:4-6) that a man should leave father and mother when he marries?

2. Indicate how each passage contradicts the notion that females are innately inferior to males:
Proverbs 1:8
Joel 2:28-29
Acts 1:14, 2:1-4
1 Peter 3:7

3. In addressing the Old Testament people of Israel, what

comparison do the prophets make regarding marriage in Isaiah 54:4-8; Jeremiah 3:14, 31:32; and Hosea 2:16?

4. What does that comparison ("repeated" in Ephesians 5:25,29,32) teach regarding submission and authority in marriage?

5. How does the "cultural mandate" (Genesis 1:28-30) still apply or not apply to both men and women today?

6. Briefly illustrate the impact of the Fall on a particular marriage you know well.

6

SELF-PROTECTIVE STRATEGIES:
Staying Safe

It is obvious to even the most casual observer that the entrance of sin into the world has made relational perfection an impossibility in this life. We may covet it because we were made for it, but our failure to measure up to our high standards of behavior (to say nothing of God's) is discouragingly regular. Consequently, the design of a loving Father that His image-bearers maintain the balance of loving authority and glad submission in marriage becomes twisted into something far different. Because of our congenital sin nature, we as marriage partners can neither submit nor love perfectly—bent as we are toward getting our own needs met in any way we can. We sense that we ought to be getting on with our God-ordained tasks of initiating and responding to each other, but in honest moments we ask ourselves: Why do I so seldom do it right?

The obvious answer, of course, is sin. I have an uncle who, whenever we're discussing an unpleasant event (a stubbed toe or too little rain), irrelevantly declares, "It's all because of sin." I suppose he's right, but as he knows, the generality utterly fails to explain anything. Similarly, it would be correct to say that sin is the reason marriages do not work, but it would also be remarkably unhelpful. Because of the

Fall, husbands do not consistently initiate with loving strength toward their wives, and wives do not always respond with trust and respect to their husbands' authority. The balance has been upset, and each partner acts in a way that is often precisely the opposite of what the other partner needs. If we are to restore things to their biblical order, we must first discern the direction of our sinning so we can begin to realign our marriages according to God's perfect design. This chapter examines how sin works to undermine the very thing each marriage partner was designed to receive and most ought to give.

SIN'S IMPACT ON MARRIAGE

When the serpent convinced Eve to disobey God and she invited Adam to join in her rebellion (Genesis 3:1-6), everything became disordered, including the marriage relationship. Satan lied when he told Eve that she and Adam would not surely die if they rebelled against God. In fact, there were deadly consequences for mankind's sin against Holy God, and as Adam's natural descendants, we suffer those consequences, too, especially in marriage.

God was true to His word. The work of death resulting from mankind's sin began at once. When God arrived for His usual fellowship with His image-bearers in the garden, He had to hunt for them in the hide-and-seek of their newfound shame and fear. Surely God knew where they were and what they had done. Yet He called out to Adam as the one responsible for the family, asking first, "Where are you?" and then, "Have you eaten from the tree that I commanded you not to eat from?" (Genesis 3:9-11). Adam, instead of acknowledging his responsibility and repenting of his failure to protect both Eve and all creation from the intrusion of evil into their world, abdicated his position. He blamed not only his wife, but indirectly the God who had given her to him. He said, "The woman you put here with me—she gave me some fruit from the tree, and I ate it" (Genesis 3:12).

God then turned to Eve and confronted her, "What is this you have done?" (Genesis 3:13). Eve should have confessed her sin of moving into the role of initiator (by listening to the serpent, choosing to disobey God, and giving some of the forbidden fruit to Adam). Instead, she blamed her failure to submit on Satan's glib tongue: "The serpent deceived me, and I ate" (Genesis 3:13).

Both image-bearers had disobeyed God's instructions entrusted to Adam (as head) to not eat the forbidden fruit (Genesis 2:16-17). But God, in confronting their transgression, told Adam his sin was that "[he] listened to [his] wife and ate from the tree" (Genesis 3:17); in other words, he followed Eve's lead instead of insisting (as initiator) that they be obedient to God. Adam's abdication of his responsible role opened the way for sin to infect the human race (Romans 5:12).

Consequently, God pronounced His righteous judgment against Adam and Eve for their rebellion. (He did not curse His image-bearers; curses were reserved for the serpent and the ground Adam would work.) The judgment against Eve (Genesis 3:16) centered on the oneness or relational aspect of their marriage, and the judgment against Adam (Genesis 3:17-19) centered on the provision or "work mandate" God had given them. The emphasis for each seems to reflect something intrinsic in their sexual nature, functions already present in their pre-Fall life together, which related to each one's greatest need.

EVE'S JUDGMENT

When God sentenced Eve for her rebellion against Heaven, He first dealt with what was uniquely female, the bearing of children. In giving birth, Eve—and all her daughters after her—would know physical pain, though she would also know thereby God's gracious gift to her of giving and sustaining life. Thus, God validated the role for which He had physically equipped Eve to begin with, that of mother and primary nurturer, even as He pronounced His judgment through that role by giving her pain in her work (they don't call it labor for nothing).

God next announced to Eve His judgment against what is certainly another important aspect of her femininity. Like all women after her, Eve had an innate need for a secure and intimate relationship with her husband in which she would be loved and cherished. Addressing that need, God told Eve that as a result of the Fall, "Your desire will be for your husband, and he will rule over you" (Genesis 3:16).

How are we to interpret the phrase "your desire will be for your husband"? Does it mean that a woman's sexual attraction (desire) for her husband is part of God's judgment against Eve for her sin? Is it true, as many have said, that sex is a result of the curse for sin? Were Adam and Eve "sexless" before they fell?

Amazingly, even in our age of supposed enlightenment regarding sexuality, many women are conditioned to believe that sex in marriage is to be endured, not enjoyed. Intercourse is considered to be a rather unpleasant duty wives owe their husbands, something to put up with as best they can in exchange for their husbands' provision and fidelity.

Fortunately, Scripture teaches sex in marriage as God's idea. Moses included it in the Creation account, its beauty is reaffirmed in the sensuous imagery of Solomon's Song of Songs, and Paul declared that sexual oneness in marriage is good. Thus, the phrase "your desire will be for your husband" cannot mean that sex is God's judgment on all women to accommodate their husbands' "animal instincts" as a cross they must bear if they intend to be married. From God's perspective, a good marriage includes mutually satisfying sexual intimacy.

What, then, does it mean that after the Fall, a woman's "desire will be for [her] husband"? This same phrase is found in Genesis 4 when God talks to Cain about his growing hatred and jealousy toward his brother, Abel. Cain is not yet guilty of mankind's first homicide, but its seeds are growing in his heart. God in love comes to speak to him about it. He warns Cain about the danger of his inner attitude: "Sin is crouching at your door; it *desires to have you,* but you must master it" (Genesis 4:7, emphasis added). The idea suggested by the phrase "it desires to have you" is that of sin desiring to have mastery over Cain. In other words, sin was out to overpower him, and Cain had to exercise his will to resist it.

In a similar way, if Eve's desire would be for her husband, it meant that her heart's intent would be to exercise mastery over Adam. Subsequent to the Fall, Eve and every other woman in her fallen state would move naturally toward control in her relationships with men, particularly her husband. As a result of sin, Eve's desire will be to control Adam, but "he will rule over [her]" (Genesis 3:16). The authority (rule) vested in Adam would counter Eve's intention and attempts to control (have mastery over) him.

God's judgment against Eve for her rebellion was not that Adam would acquire a ruling position over her, but that his already existent authority would make them competitive instead of complementary. Their formerly joyous obedience to their "cultural mandate"—with Adam initiating as leader and Eve gladly responding as helper—would henceforth be a struggle to decide who was in charge.

What had been held in perfect balance was going to be "out of sync," a sad and inevitable conflict of wills. Because Eve would no longer feel assured that Adam's decisions would be made with her best interest in mind, she would try to fight for her rights. Because Adam would feel threatened by her criticism or attempts to control him, he would contend against her to maintain his authority over her. Their oneness was sundered, their mutual security in each other's love broken. And Eve would experience, more keenly than Adam, that aspect of their fallenness.

ADAM'S JUDGMENT

Adam received God's judgment for his chosen abdication to Eve's "leadership" into sin in the area of his work, his tilling of the soil. He would receive the gracious gift of being able to provide for his family (an intrinsic part of his maleness), but it would cost him the sweat of his brow and painful toil in the fields that once had gladly yielded their increase to his efforts. His adequacy to handle his world was undermined by the ground's resistance to his attempts at cultivation. Mastery over the earth was no longer assured, and with that lack of assurance came a debilitating loss of the confidence he had once felt to provide for his wife. Adam surely was affected by God's judgment against Eve in the area of relationship (just as she was affected by God's judgment against him in the area of his work), but Adam's loss of guaranteed significance through successful labor as a strong man able to care for his wife would influence him more than it would Eve.

BARRIERS

For both Adam and Eve, the "LORD God made garments of skin . . . and clothed them" (Genesis 3:21). This act was not a part of God's judgment on them; rather, He was exhibiting kindness toward them. The compassionate Father graciously clothed His now consciously naked image-bearers. This necessary wardrobe for His sin-embarrassed children was a symbol of the continuing shame they would feel for their nakedness—emotional as well as physical. That shame would cause them to avert their eyes from the divine One whose love never wavered, and it would also cause them to avert their eyes from the human one whose love could not be counted on anymore.

Just as garments of animal skin covered their bodies, there were unseen garments layered over their hurting hearts as well. They had hidden from God in the garden when He came to walk with them in the cool of the day, and now they would also hide from each other, even (perhaps especially) in their most intimate encounters. What had once been unabashed openness with each other had now become a fearful uncertainty behind which both hid from the other the true desires and needs of their hearts. They would be strangers because they could no longer trust absolutely in the other's perfect love and care. They might even become enemies, each holding the greatest power to hurt the other—exactly because of their intimate relationship. One thing was certain: No longer would they be able to live without their protective coverings.

Self-Protection

The sad truth is that all of us, whether single or married, have inherited from our first parents this same innate proclivity to protect ourselves. Though we were designed as marriage partners to meet each other's need for love and respect, we find that instead we come to marriage demanding that our own needs be met to protect ourselves from being disappointed. Husbands demand that wives submit to their authority and respect them—no matter what. Wives demand that husbands love them strongly and sacrificially—no matter what. Even when by God's grace we try to meet His standards for appropriately loving a spouse, there is often a hidden agenda with the twin goals of getting the other person to meet our needs ("I'm being godly so you'd better treat me right") and protecting ourselves from being hurt ("I'm behaving right so don't criticize or reject me in any way").

All people bring to marriage unique methods of self-protection, fine-tuned to counteract the particular disappointments and fears of earlier experiences. Having not been perfectly loved and valued in childhood (no one ever could be), people somehow expect their marriages to be different. They look forward to the interest, concern, attentiveness, and romance that characterized the courtship. Sometime after the wedding, however, when the relationship has become more routine, more settled, both discover that expectations don't always match up with reality. He is not as strong and loving as she had thought he would be, and she is not as affirming and available as he had expected her to be.

The Intrusion of Fear

At this point in a marriage certain fears and disappointments from earlier relationships begin to stir, often unconsciously. She fears that he will let her down as her father or her former boyfriend did, and she desperately does not want to go through that pain again. He suspects that maybe she will not really admire him but will criticize and undermine his adequacy the way his mother did to his father for so many years. What is now at the heart of the relationship between these two marriage partners is not love or respect; it's fear—fear of disappointment, fear of failure, fear of being hurt again.

Fear has an insidious way of canceling out love. Throughout Scripture, God expresses His love to His children by telling them, "Fear not." He knew that as long as their hearts were governed by fear (of their enemies, of their circumstances, of their future), they could not respond in faith and love toward Him or one another.

Fear is rooted in uncertainty—first about God's sovereignty and goodness toward us, and then about how others will treat us. Love, on the other hand, is rooted in faith that God is both sovereign and good (despite what the circumstances might suggest to the contrary) and that we can expect good from His hand, regardless of how we are being treated by those around us. Fear and love will always contest for dominance in the human heart, whether in relationship to God or to other people. Fear and love are mutually incompatible.

Learning to Hide

When fear takes over in a marriage, a predictable phenomenon occurs that reflects exactly what happened in the Garden of Eden after Adam and Eve rebelled against God. The first thing they did after realizing their sin was to sew fig leaves together and make coverings for themselves (Genesis 3:7). Their fear of God and of each other made them instinctively want to hide. Fig leaves were not particularly in fashion nor were they exactly an effective covering, but Adam and Eve knew they needed protection from each other.

Husbands and wives have always done the same thing when they were afraid of each other, not always with physical covering (though sometimes they do literally hide), but with tactics designed to control or to evade the other person. Let's examine how that might look in a contemporary marriage.

AN EXAMPLE OF MARITAL SELF-PROTECTION

Steve and Kerri, the couple described in the first chapter, thought for many years they had a good marriage. Kerri truly desired to be submissive to Steve's leadership, but she soon began to sense he was not the strong man she needed and had thought him to be during their whirlwind courtship. When a decision had to be made, he depended on her input too much in order to decide, and he usually ended up doing what she wanted.

At first that felt good to Kerri; he seemed to respect her and have her best interest in mind. But once when a certain decision had to be made, she left it entirely up to him. For over a week Steve could not decide, and eventually, the stress of his uncertainty became too much for Kerri to handle. She gave him a little clue about what to do, and he gratefully made his decision.

Kerri's worst fears had been realized, though she was unaware of it at the time. Subconsciously, she had always been afraid of being disappointed again (as she had been with her alcoholic father) and left without a strong, emotionally involved man she could respect and depend on. So she pretended Steve was stronger than he was, unconsciously taking up the slack in his withdrawal from leadership. *She became the strong one in the family*, the rock on whom Steve and the children could depend. Instead of extending to him her trust that he could manage things, Kerri essentially emasculated Steve and undermined the very self-esteem she wished he had. She was afraid he would let her down and emotionally abandon her (especially if his drinking got worse). And her strategy, far from being the godly submission she desired and believed she was practicing, was to control everything and protect herself from being hurt. Because her take-charge approach was quiet and sweet, it went unrecognized as the manipulation it actually was. But self-protective fear, not love, motivated her.

And Steve was not being gently strong. He was scared to death he might make a mistake or Kerri might disapprove of him and maybe even emotionally abandon him as his mother had done. He was afraid to risk being the leader she needed him to be because he had too often risked and failed. He did not think he could survive more failure. His motivation in seeking Kerri's advice was not love (concern for her welfare) but fear (concern for his own). Without knowing how or why, he was letting her down in a significant way with regard to her need for strong, loving leadership. Steve's real shortcoming was a failure to love, rooted in the fear that he was not (perhaps could not be) the man she needed and he wanted to be.

SELF-PROTECTION PERVERTS GOD'S DESIGN

What was happening in the inner life of this marriage, unrecognized by both Kerri and Steve, occurs with unfortunate regularity in marriages throughout the Christian community. Fear-powered strategies to protect themselves from each other drive both partners farther and farther from the ministry to which God has called them in marriage. What each spouse does to stay safe is a perversion of and counterproductive to the "tasks" each one is designed by God to accomplish for the sake of the other.

Consider the perversion. The husband is intended to be strong and loving, an involved leader for his wife and family. However, when he fails to be that and his wife capitulates to her fear, she usually moves in and takes control. A wife's control is the perversion of her husband's leadership (which should never control), a travesty of the kind of authority God expects a husband to lovingly exercise for his wife's benefit and well-being. It is also the opposite of the submission the wife is called to exercise toward her husband. Whether it is overt or subtle, a wife's control is sensed as being somehow out of sync with how things ought to be, because it mimics in a perverted way her husband's God-ordained role as initiator.

Or a woman might use her submission to keep from taking appropriate responsibility for her life, thereby allowing herself the luxury of letting her husband take the blame for every family decision (especially the ones that turn out poorly). Like the fearful servant, she digs a hole and hides her "talent" for fear of making a mistake (Matthew 25:14-30).

Such "submission," such backing away from being a whole person vitally involved in responding to her husband, is a perversion of the active—even aggressive—responsiveness to Christ that the Church is called to evidence. In speaking to the indifference of the first-century Christians at Laodicea, Christ announced to them through the Apostle John, "I know your deeds, that you are neither cold nor hot. I wish you were either one or the other! So, because you are lukewarm—neither hot nor cold—I am about to spit you out of my mouth" (Revelation 3:15-16). A wife's indifference masquerading as submission in marriage disgusts the Savior in the same way as does the Church's indifference to her first love.

It is also a perversion of God's model for marriage when a husband capitulates to his fear that his wife might criticize or reject his leadership. He retreats behind the newspaper or a busy schedule or a cheerful indifference or an emotional distance he refuses to gulf; his avenues of retreat are many and varied. A husband's self-protective weakness is the perversion of womanly submission, which should be neither retreating nor weak, and it happens whenever a husband runs from involvement with his wife out of his fear of failing as a man. It is also the opposite of the leadership he is called by God to exercise in his family.

Or perhaps the husband exercises his authority in a cruel and abusive way, attempting to control his wife to meet his need for mastery or personal comfort. When he fails to use his authority to lay down his life for her with sacrificial *agape* love, he perverts that authority into a self-serving power play. He imitates the Gentile rulers whose leadership style Christ contrasted with His model of servanthood (Matthew 20:25-28). This twisted expression of authority may be the expected thing to persons who are of the world, but Jesus vehemently opposed it. Self-protection by either husband or wife inevitably leads to a perversion of the husband-wife roles in marriage.

SELF-PROTECTION DOES NOT WORK

Moreoever, self-protective strategies are counterproductive. They do not accomplish what either the husband or the wife intends to accomplish. For example, I didn't improve my chances of being strongly loved when I self-protectively moved in to control things by telling Bill how to handle his job, how to relate to our son, what to say to make me feel good, and so on and so on. A wife's control may intimidate her husband so that he backs away (the opposite of the strength she desires), or it may anger him and push him to fight back to maintain his authority (the opposite of the love she needs). The husband is not to be excused for his sinful withdrawal or unkindness, but the point is that the wife does not get what she wants when she abandons her role and takes charge. Her unsubmissiveness is counterproductive to the loving involvement she really wants.

The barometer wife, who abandons her personhood to keep herself safe, does not get what she really wants, either. Instead of being esteemed and valued by her husband for her God-given uniqueness, a wife who refuses to take responsibility for her life invites her husband to invest in other relationships for his personal growth and enrichment. Again, he cannot be justified for abandoning her emotionally, but her choice to find her life and identity only in her husband is counterproductive to her desire for his interested, loving involvement with her.

Similarly, the husband who retreats from his wife (abandoning his leadership role) fails to earn the respect he desires from her. When Bill's fear of my rejection, for example, moves him self-protectively away from involvement with me, he encourages me to move in to take up the slack—the very manipulation he fears and hates. Again, my sinful control is not excusable on the basis of his retreat. But a husband's abdication of his God-given authority works in direct opposition to the very respect and trust he wants from his wife. His fearful uninvolvement is counterproductive to the submission and responsiveness he deeply desires.

When a husband resorts to cruelty or power plays to protect himself from feeling out of control of his world, he may earn his wife's "obedience," but never her respect. If she "submits" to his bullying, he will get no genuine satisfaction because her "submission" will be rooted in her fear, not her trust; therefore, it will not affirm his manhood. What he deeply wants from her (her trust and respect) he cannot gain for himself by strong-arm tactics.

SUMMING UP

Thus, self-protection, which is the opposite of love, lies at the heart of mankind's every relationship difficulty, especially within marriage. When the motivation behind submissive behavior or the exercise of authority is fear (of rejection, disapproval, disrespect, or whatever), the result is always self-protection, which is sin because it represents a failure to love. Love is other-directed, but self-protection focuses on the self. To the degree that I am concerned to protect myself, to that degree I am unable to be involved in loving anyone else.

An infinite variety of self-protective behaviors are available to marriage partners, limited only by the creativity of our fallen nature. I most often self-protectively control my situation by basically writing the script for Bill's life, by being the leader in a group, or by staying busy, preferably with "spiritual" activities like church work or my writing. Bill usually self-protects by backing away from decisions or looking for someone to blame when things go wrong.

We all have unique strategies for self-protection, but whatever they are, God's command is that we face them as the sin He has named them to be and move toward repentance and change. The next chapter will examine God's design for redeemed marriages—what husbands and wives are intended to give to each other that goes directly counter to their inclination toward self-protection.

QUESTIONS FOR THOUGHT AND DISCUSSION

1. Comment on this statement: Eve's sin was in initiating instead of responding to Adam's leadership, and Adam's sin was in responding to Eve instead of to God.

2. What do you fear that makes you want to protect yourself personally (emotionally, not just physically)?

3. How do you usually protect yourself from hurt?

4. Explain why your self-protection is or is not working.

5. How do you think God perceives your self-protection?

7

BALANCING ACT:
Meeting Needs

If we compare the model of marriage presented to us in the early chapters of Genesis with the ways in which husbands and wives live out their marriages today, the effects of the Fall become painfully apparent. Yet because of the cross of Christ, it is possible for redeemed image-bearers to live a new way in all relationships, particularly marriage. Instead of self-protection and self-seeking, believers are called to "submit to one another out of reverence for Christ" in response to the filling of the Holy Spirit (Ephesians 5:18-21). In other words, they are to discover the needs of their fellow believers and then do what they can to meet those needs because of their commitment to Jesus. The instruction is clearly intended for all believers, but Paul goes on to show how that submission should work itself out in specific relationships, beginning with marriage.

The *NIV Study Bible* says *submit* means "to yield one's own rights,"[1] and the clear assumption is that wives as well as husbands possess rights that they can choose to yield according to the other's legitimate needs. But the person submitting must know what the other person's needs are in order to know in what context to yield his or her rights. If the balance of submission and authority in marriage is to be genuine and biblical, we must first ask what husbands and wives were created to give and to receive in marriage as God designed it.

DISCERNING LEGITIMATE NEEDS

Though Jesus left no specific instructions regarding married life, by what He did and taught He elevated both the status of women and the sanctity of the one-man-one-woman-for-life marriage bond. Paul, however, specifically taught how believers should behave in their marriages by listing the duties owed by Christian wives to their husbands and Christian husbands to their wives (Ephesians 5:22-33). By examining that passage, we can discern what a husband needs from his wife and what a wife needs from her husband. Thus, it is possible to identify the needs each has for which the other is to yield rights.

UNDERLYING ASSUMPTIONS

Paul begins by reaffirming (or, perhaps more accurately, reassuming) the structure God built into the social order of marriage, which is the initiating position of the husband and the responsive role of the wife to his authority. Paul does not argue the husband's authority; he merely assumes it (as he does in Colossians 3:18 and Titus 2:5; as does Peter in 1 Peter 3:1). Paul's instructions to wives and husbands are to be examined in the context of that assumed structure, created by God for maintaining balance in the marriage relationship.

Another assumption Paul made was that his Christian readers could actually obey his instructions regarding marriage, though they seem to hit at the very heart of what is most difficult for both men and women to do. Certainly those instructions did not reflect Jewish or Graeco-Roman first-century culture. The women of Paul's day had virtually no choice about submitting, except as it concerned their attitude, and the men were unaccustomed to fidelity, let alone sacrificial love.

Paul, like Jesus Christ, refused to be limited by contemporary social or religious expectations. Instead he lifted up and modeled the way men and women were designed and called to treat each other. In doing so, both Jesus and Paul affirmed that God's relationship designs were correct and doable, though only through the Spirit's power.

Because we are redeemed image-bearers, it is possible for husbands and wives to live out our Holy Spirit regeneration by choosing to obey the submit-love instructions of Scripture (particularly in Ephesians 5). We have needs that, because of the Spirit's filling, can be met by each other within marriage. Let's consider what Paul indicated those needs were.

A HUSBAND'S NEEDS

Paul begins this section on marriage by speaking to wives about their marital obligations:

> Wives, submit to your husbands as to the Lord. For the husband is the head of the wife as Christ is the head of the church, his body, of which he is the Savior. Now as the church submits to Christ, so also wives should submit to their husbands in everything. (Ephesians 5:22-24)

He sums up his advice to wives by saying that "the wife must respect her husband" (verse 33).

From these verses (and from the Creation account), we can draw some conclusions as to what a husband needs that his wife is called on to provide for him. From the Creation story, we can conclude that he needs a woman of substance, a suitable helper who will respond to his leadership as he initiates to subdue and populate the earth. Adam (even after the Fall) would have been disappointed if Eve had refused to engage with him as his partner in the work God had called both of them to do. He did not need a slave; he needed a woman who knew who she was and was confident in her gifts. An alive, vibrant woman gives zest and excitement to her husband's life. He needs that.

But that is not all he needs. Ephesians 5:22-24 indicates that a husband also desires this capable and confident wife to be willing to submit to his authority. What does it mean for her to submit?

THE MEANING OF SUBMISSION

Sometimes it is easier to define a term by describing what it is *not* before exploring what it *is*. Submission does not imply a wife's obedience or slavery; she ought not to become a nonperson who exists only to grant her husband's wishes. In addition to defining submission as the yielding of one's rights, the *NIV Study Bible* states of Ephesians 5:22,

> If the relationship called for it, as in the military, the term could connote obedience, but that meaning is not called for here. In fact, the word "obey" does not appear in Scripture with respect to wives, though it does with respect to children (6:1) and slaves (6:5).

Furthermore, marital submission does not make a wife an extension of her husband, nor does it make him an extension of her, for that matter. A submissive wife is not called to close her eyes to her husband's faults as though they do not exist, nor is she required to have sex with her husband whenever he feels like it. It certainly does not mean she ought to patiently take abuse, physical or verbal. She does not have to commit intellectual suicide; she should feel free to think her thoughts and offer her opinion on any issue. Moreover, a wife need not necessarily deny herself the option of using her giftedness in a job outside the home—considering, of course, how that would affect her obligations to her family. These are some of the things submission does *not* mean.

It is more difficult to define what submission in marriage *does* mean. The word translated "subject" or "submit" in Ephesians 5:22-24 is the Greek word *hupotasso,* which is "primarily a military term, to rank under."[2] *Hupotasso* is comprised of two parts, *hupo* (under) and *tasso* (to arrange). Thus a valid translation of the word would be "to arrange or order oneself under the authority of another." *Hupotasso* assumes an authority, implied or stated, in every New Testament text in which it is found.

A husband needs his wife to be willing to place herself under his leadership in the family, gladly and without a critical spirit. She must be strong, but she must also bring her strength into place under his headship and initiation. She must respond to his strength, not just lean on her own. A man needs his wife to risk trusting his adequacy to lead and provide for the family in the same way the Church trusts Christ to serve as her head and guide. A husband must know his wife is willing to receive his strength and to depend on him for support and encouragement in their life together.

Integral to a wife's submission is her respect for her husband as a man. She is to truly honor him from her heart. A wife who disdains or demeans or emasculates her husband (and there are infinite ways to do it) violates the essence of a submissive spirit. When a man finds a wife who will gladly respond to his leadership and consistently show her respect for him, he has found a rare gem if she is also a woman of substance and feminine strength.

CAUTIONS REGARDING SUBMISSION

This does not mean a woman's husband should become her god or replace Christ in her life. A footnote in the *NIV Study Bible* states that the phrase "*as to the Lord* [d]oes not put a woman's husband in the place of the Lord, but shows rather that a woman ought to submit to her husband as an act of submission to the Lord."[3] If a woman deeply desires to place her life under the lordship of Jesus, she must also be willing to submit to the headship of her husband as part of her submission to Christ.

Moreover, a wife's submission is to be unconditional. She must show a willingness to appropriately depend on and respect her husband, even when he is not being all that she needs him to be for her. In the footnote to Ephesians 5:23 in the *NIV Study Bible,* we are reminded, "Christ earned, so to speak, the right to his special relationship to the church."[4] Just so, a husband cannot demand but must seek to show himself deserving of his wife's submission. However, in spite of how well or poorly he is following Christ's example, she must evidence a genuine *willingness* to submit to him and to trust his leadership. If he abdicates that authority, she must know how to deal with that reality while still showing him heartfelt respect.

Those, then, are the needs every husband has, and the wife is called and uniquely equipped to minister to those needs. In a later chapter, we will examine how she can do so, even when he is failing her.

A WIFE'S NEEDS

What does a woman need that her husband is uniquely designed to fulfill? From the Creation account, we can conclude that she needs to be recognized as his equal before God, equally valuable, equally the recipient of God's gifts (though the gifts will differ), equally "one in Christ Jesus" (Galatians 3:28), and equally "heirs . . . of the gracious gift of life" (1 Peter 3:7). Her value is no less than his, her needs no less important than his. She needs to know, even in the context of God's declaration that a woman's husband "will rule over [her]" (Genesis 3:16), that her husband esteems her equally with himself.

When Paul penned his instructions to husbands in Ephesians 5, he gave them a longer list of requirements than he gave to wives. If it was difficult for the women of Paul's day (in which men were generally cruel to and exploitive of women) to biblically submit to their husbands, it was equally difficult for those men to biblically love their wives.

The men in the churches to which Paul was writing had a view of marriage (and of women in general) far different from ours and far different from Paul's. Dr. James Hurley, in his book *Man and Woman in Biblical Perspective,* summarized first-century Jewish, Roman, and Greek attitudes toward women: "Without exception, the cultures . . . assumed male leadership and legal responsibility. . . . From the evidence which we possess it would seem that women were often considered to be inferior, not only with respect to legal rights, but also as human beings."[5]

In other words, Jews, Greeks, and Romans of the New Testament era regarded women and marriage with considerably less esteem than did either Jesus or Paul. The rights of first-century women were virtually nonexistent, even among the Jews. A husband could dissolve his marriage almost at will. The custom of men playing musical marriages was so common then that even Jesus' disciples were shocked when He declared that one-woman-one-man-for-life was God's intention (Matthew 19:3-11). Permanence in marriage was as unpopular in that day as it is in our own, only without the legal provisions for wives afforded by our contemporary laws.

Against the backdrop of the power that husbands in Paul's audience exercised over their wives and the selfish "freedom" they were accustomed to in their marriages, listen as *they* might have listened to what Paul said their wives needed and they were required to provide:

Husbands, love your wives, just as Christ loved the church and gave himself up for her to make her holy, cleansing her by the washing with water through the word, and to present her to himself as a radiant church, without stain or wrinkle or any other blemish, but holy and blameless. In this same way, husbands ought to love their wives as their own bodies. He who loves his wife loves himself. After all, no one ever hated his own body, but he feeds and cares for it, just as Christ does the church—for we are members of his body. (Ephesians 5:25-30)

What a picture this passage provides of a strong man moving toward his wife to initiate whatever is for her benefit! Far from allowing Christian husbands to exercise their authority by "bossing" their wives around or getting rid of them because of some irritation, Paul told them to love their wives as much as they loved themselves, to sacrificially lay down their lives for them as Christ did for His Church.

The men must have been shocked by Paul's comments. Perhaps they were thinking what the disciples were thinking when they responded to Jesus' teaching on permanent monogamy by saying, "If this is the situation between a husband and wife, it is better not to marry" (Matthew 19:10). These husbands were handed a tall order: No matter what your wife is like, even when she is not responding as you wish she would, love her with *agape* love the way Jesus loved His Church. Even in the best of marriages, it would be no easy task.

SACRIFICIAL LOVE DEFINED

The conclusion we can draw from Paul's instructions to husbands in Ephesians 5 is that wives most need their husbands' sacrificial love (loving their wives "as Christ loved the church and gave himself up for her" [verse 25]). This model of strong yet gentle authority exercised in selfless love plays itself out in three of a wife's more particular needs: for her husband's spiritual leadership (giving himself up "to make her holy" [verse 26]), for his careful provision (as he "feeds" his own body [verse 29]), and for his protective cherishing (as he "cares for" his own body [verse 29]). That kind of confident husbandly movement toward intimate involvement with his chosen partner was undoubtedly rare among the married men to whom Paul wrote (it is equally rare today), but it certainly speaks to the heart of almost every woman I know.

Consider Paul's statement that husbands must exercise their God-given authority by loving their wives as themselves. J.B. Phillips translates it this way: "Men ought to give their wives the love they naturally have for their own bodies. The love a man gives his wife is the extending of his love for himself to enfold her." Paul rightly declares that a man never hates his own body, though he may dislike certain physical traits or the condition his body is in at any given moment. Monsignor Ronald Knox in his translation says, "It is unheard of, that a man should bear ill-will to his own flesh." Self-love comes naturally, and Paul suggests that this very love for self is what a husband should extend in a wide circle that "enfolds" his wife.

So often the discussion of submission in marriage centers on how a wife ought to act toward her husband. Certainly the Christian women I know (myself included) struggle to understand and implement a genuinely submissive spirit—both toward God and toward our husbands. But if Paul's model is imitated, there should be at least equal emphasis placed on the command that husbands initiate love toward their wives with an increasingly selfless and other-centered concern. The wife's willing submission must be equally balanced by the sacrificial loving of her husband if God's design is to "work."

Far too many Christian men are more invested in the quality of their wives' submission than in the quality of their own loving. Surely there are exceptions, but the bentness of fallen human nature prevents even committed Christian husbands from recognizing just how much their wives need for them to imitate Jesus' sacrificial abandonment to His Bride's welfare.

Every woman longs to have this unselfish concern for her good from a strong and loving man. Most women think they have found that when they are being courted, and they grieve most for that kind of caring when the dailiness of marriage replaces the exhilaration of the honeymoon. Every woman wants to be loved as Jesus loves His Church, with strength and commitment. And that is what Paul called husbands to do in their marriages.

Spiritual Leadership
Three aspects of sacrificial love are detailed in this passage. First, a Christian husband is to show concern for his wife's spiritual welfare by providing spiritual leadership in the home. Ephesians 5:26-27 describes Christ's deep regard for His Church. He died to cleanse her

from sin and to present her to Himself as righteous and unblemished. The *New English Bible* states that Christ "loved the church and gave himself up for it, to consecrate it" (5:25). God's particular love for human beings as His image-bearers (referred to in this passage as Christ's love for His Church) speaks primarily to their need for spiritual renewal in their relationship with the God who created them. And because Christ's love for His Church is also the model for a husband's love for his wife, any Christian marriage in which the husband has nothing to do with the spiritual well-being of his wife and children falls short of modeling Christ's concern for His Church.

That is not to say that a husband is the savior of his family, though a Christian man must intercede daily for his wife and children. Ultimately, each person must answer to God for individual spiritual decisions. A husband's spiritual responsibility for his family does mean that God will hold him accountable for the way his prayer life, his priorities, the spiritual instruction of his family in God's Word, and his own example of love and godliness have been used to lead his family toward a closer walk with God. Providing spiritual leadership and nurturing his wife's spiritual life indicate a man's sacrificial love.

Careful Provision
A second aspect of a husband's sacrificial love for his wife is in his careful provision for her. Paul reminds his male readers that every man "feeds and cares for" his own body (Ephesians 5:29), and husbands should be that diligent in regard to their wives. A husband ought to provide for his family's material needs as best he can; being a good provider is one of his richest ways to express and experience his adequacy to strongly love his wife.

God seems to have assumed as much when He spoke specifically to Adam's physical provision for Eve when pronouncing judgment for Adam's sin (Genesis 3:19). Evidently, it dealt with his essential contribution to the well-being of Eden—that is, the procurement of physical sustenance for his family. Some of the persistent questions of today's Western culture address this very issue: Must the husband be the primary or only breadwinner in the family? Is the house-husband concept a violation of Scripture? What if the wife makes more money than the husband?

The traditional model of a wife staying home with the children while her husband earns a living for them is increasingly rare, and the reasons are many and varied. Economic necessity, emphasis on a higher standard of living, and the desire for personal fulfillment through career opportunities for women all contribute to the husband's decreasing identification as sole provider for the family. But if God's design was that the husband move with strength and initiation into the relationship with his wife and that the wife relate as responder and helper, then surely the balance is upset when the wife becomes the strong one who plans and provides for the family instead of looking to the husband for that kind of leadership. Moreover, a woman who takes over the material provision of the family tends toward exerting influence in other areas as well.

This is not to say that a woman should never have a job. Some families cannot survive in today's economy without her help. But the pursuit of a full-time career by many women often flows not from financial necessity but from their sense of not having had their needs adequately met through their roles as wives and mothers. I understand the temptation. Many times during the past few years I have "escaped" to my writing when I didn't want to face the problems in my relationship with Bill that day.

On a larger scale, when marriage and motherhood do not satisfy, a woman may seek fulfillment through a career rather than deal with the pain of her unmet needs. Working for the family's good is not the same as working because of the family's deficit. A Christian wife must be careful not to abandon her role as wife and primary nurturer or refuse to receive from her husband what he desires to give her—his commitment to "feed" or nourish her. And the husband must be careful not to demand that she take over or augment his role as provider just so they can enjoy a higher standard of living. What should be more important than their level of income is their unwillingness to compromise his role as leader-initiator and hers as helper-responder in the marriage.

A husband's provision encompasses more than just caring for his wife's physical needs. Instead of translating the Greek as "feeds," the *King James Version* uses "nourisheth," which implies responsibility for other kinds of provision as well. A wife needs to be able to depend on her husband to also nourish her mentally, emotionally, and spiritually, because she is more than just a physical being. When a man makes provision for his wife to be the best-educated, most well-adjusted, and most spiritually mature woman she can possibly be, he is fulfilling his mandate to nourish her as he would his own body. To do less (especially if his motive is selfish or self-protective) is to ignore the example of Christ, who has selflessly provided for and encouraged the development and exercise of each believer's giftedness. A husband should want his wife to be all that she can be. It is part of loving her sacrificially.

Protective Cherishing

A third aspect of a husband's selfless love is that he "cares for" or protectively cherishes (KJV) his wife (Ephesians 5:29). As a husband treats his body, so he should also treat his wife. He should look for ways to let her know she is special to him, his unique rose among all other flowers in the world. A woman never tires of being shown that she is cherished; it speaks deeply to her heart.

But *cherish* also implies that a husband must shield or cover his wife protectively to keep her from harm—and not just physical injury. She needs him to guard her emotionally from unjust criticism and verbal abuse, especially his own. She also has a deep need for the safety of her inner personhood. Her self-image and sense of personal worth are to be under his tender care and encouragement so that she need not look outside the marriage for emotional intimacy. And a husband must be committed to guard his wife sexually from physical attack as well as from more subtle verbal or mental assault on her purity by other men.

He is to keep special watch over his life and thoughts so that she need not fear that most destructive of all attacks, her own husband's emotional or sexual abandonment of her for another lover. Protecting the sanctity of the emotional and sexual intimacy of his relationship with his wife should be his top priority, just as Jesus' fidelity to His Church is unquestioned.

Though a wife's unwarranted jealousy has the power to seriously damage the marriage, there is also an appropriate marital jealousy that reflects God's jealous love for His people. In *Submission Is for Husbands, Too* Mark Littleton defined *godly jealousy* as "the desire to protect from interference a relationship that is precious and intimate. No husband or wife should stand by and let a third party intrude on the intimacy that is reserved for them alone."[6] If a husband is sacrificially loving his wife by cherishing her, she will know herself safe with him in all areas in which she needs his protection.

THE MUTUAL GIFT OF INTIMACY

When both husband and wife minister to each other according to God's creation design before the Fall and according to God's redemptive design as described by Paul, then the sexual intimacy that binds husband and wife exclusively to each other evidences what Paul reaffirmed in Ephesians 5:31 (quoted from Genesis 2:24): "For this reason a man will leave his father and mother and be united to his wife, and the two will become one flesh."

The "one flesh" experience of sexual union is the natural expression and reflection of the spiritual and emotional oneness already present in the marriage relationship. This is not to say that marriage partners will be able to have satisfying and exciting sex simply because they are married, regardless of past experience or teaching (or lack of the same). But it certainly affirms that enjoying sex is a legitimate goal in marriage and worth the time and effort it may take for either or both partners to overcome inhibitions and strive to improve. In the context of a commitment to marital love, sexual intimacy can be all that God meant it to be, the joyous expression of deep personal union between two of God's image-bearers.

AS CHRIST LOVES THE CHURCH

The intimacy and intertwining of two separate entities (husband and wife) into one is a glorious and wonderful paradox—distinctly two becoming distinctively one. Paul closed his instructions to husbands and wives with this startling conclusion: "This is a profound mystery— but I am talking about Christ and the church" (Ephesians 5:32). How could something as ordinary as marriage reflect something as extraordinary as the intimate involvement of the infinite Creator with His finite creatures? The commonplace is to transcend its own boundaries and leap beyond itself into the eternal and spiritual nature of all things. Paul was right. This is mystery indeed. And even more mind-boggling, we have to wonder how finite human beings can ever hope to adequately emulate (as husbands) or return (as wives) the perfect love of an infinitely loving God toward His people. Can it be done?

Surely not perfectly; we still live in a fallen world. But just as surely we are called to respond in obedience to God's command. We are called not to the impossible dream but to the hard work of redeemed living in our marriages. We can learn to live by grace, forgiven and forgiving of our imperfect spouses. Part of what it means to live holy lives before God as re-created image-bearers is that we are called to— and equipped for—excellence in marriage. Knowing each other's needs as husbands and wives, we must commit ourselves to drawing on the infinite resources of God through the Holy Spirit to meet those needs as best we can.

SUMMING UP

What, then, are the needs of a husband and a wife that each can meet for the other, according to Genesis and Ephesians? A husband needs his wife's self-confidence and glad willingness to respect him and submit to his leadership. His wife needs his esteem and his strong, sacrificial love, which involves spiritual leadership, careful provision, and protective cherishing so that she will know herself deeply valued as a woman. Marriage is a delicate balancing act in which each partner must yield—first to the order of authority God established and then to each one's individual responsibility to submit within that order.

What a list! Its idealism forces us to reevaluate the inner dynamics of our own marriages to see why they are not working any better than they are. We must stop hiding from each other and ourselves (as Adam and Eve hid from God in the garden) and take an honest look at our styles of self-protection. Our fear of being hurt often blinds us to the ways we ought to meet our spouses' needs, and we become consumed with *getting* rather than *giving* in our marriages. In his rush to be respected, the husband neglects to love, and in her hurry to be loved, his wife neglects to submit. Or her "submission" and his "love" become games they play while they get on with their *real* agenda, which is to protect themselves from feeling inadequate or rejected and to somehow get their own needs met. In the next chapter, we will look at what it means to repent as husbands and wives of the sin of self-protective "authority" and "submission."

NOTES:
1. *The NIV Study Bible,* Kenneth Barker ed. (Grand Rapids: Zondervan Bible Publishers, 1985), page 1798.
2. W.E. Vine, "hupotasso," *Vine's Expository Dictionary of Old and New Testament*

Words, vol. 4 (Old Tappan, N.J.: Fleming H. Revell, 1981), page 86.
3. The NIV Study Bible, page 1798.
4. The NIV Study Bible, page 1798.
5. James B. Hurley, Man and Woman in Biblical Perspective (Grand Rapids: Zondervan Publishing House, 1981), page 77.
6. Mark R. Littleton, Submission Is for Husbands, Too (Denver, Colo.: Accent Books, 1988), page 157.

QUESTIONS FOR THOUGHT AND DISCUSSION

1. Read the passages listed below. Then show how Ruth fulfilled Boaz's needs according to Paul's instructions in Ephesians 5:22-24.

Ruth 1:16
Ruth 2:13
Ruth 3:5
Ruth 3:9

2. Based on the passages below, explain how Boaz met Ruth's needs according to Paul's instructions in Ephesians 5:25-30.

Ruth 2:1
Ruth 2:8-9
Ruth 2:11
Ruth 2:12
Ruth 2:14
Ruth 3:11
Ruth 3:14
Ruth 4:13

3. Name several practical ways a wife can show genuine respect for her husband.

4. Identify ways a husband can nourish his wife mentally, emotionally, and spiritually.

5. How can a husband protect his wife emotionally, personally, and sexually?

8

GENUINE REPENTANCE:
Embracing a New Purpose

If it is true that the fundamental sin in our marriages is that we fearfully seek safety behind our masks of "authority" and "submission" rather than endeavor to meet our spouses' need for love and respect, then the fundamental antidote for repairing our broken relationships must be genuine repentance for our self-protection. What does it mean to repent of self-protection?

The verb *repent* "signifies to change one's mind or purpose."[1] Thus, to repent in our marriages means that we discover and acknowledge the sin of depending not on God but on our unique strategies for protecting ourselves from our spouses. Then we must deliberately change our old purpose (self-sufficiency and self-protection) and live out a new purpose (trust in God and love and respect for our spouses) in line with God's intent. Marital repentance involves admitting the sinfulness of our safe-seeking methods and embracing dependence on God and openness (the opposite of self-protection) in our relationships with our marriage partners.

Before examining what it means to acknowledge and grieve over our self-protection, we must distinguish between wrong and right reasons to repent. Or to say it another way, we must define sin.

REPENTING OF THE WRONG THINGS

Sometimes our mistake is not in repenting too seldom or too insincerely, but in repenting of the wrong things.

God never intended for us to minimize the fear of pain and disappointment that motivates us to protect ourselves in the first place. He knows the fear is legitimate and the pain is real. Some believers feel guilty for wanting to be loved or respected; they think they are unspiritual for needing the affection or trust of their mates. But they must learn to differentiate between their legitimate desire for intimate love and their sinful, self-protective attempts to procure that love apart from God through their own devices. It is a mistake to repent of longings for intimacy, but altogether appropriate to repent of safe-seeking strategies to get those longings satisfied.

All men and women have a God-given capacity for genuine love and significance. From the beginning, God intended for that capacity to be filled, first of all through our relationship with Him. As Augustine pointed out, God created us for Himself, and our hearts are restless until they find rest in Him. God intends for us to allow our legitimate fear and pain to drive us to Him so that we ultimately find our inner life in Him alone. Our deepest peace comes from resting in God's love revealed through Jesus in the midst of disappointing circumstances, receiving His grace and abiding in Him daily. That is where real life is—hidden in God.

This capacity for experiencing God's love is the basis for what Jesus called the "first and greatest" commandment: "Love the Lord your God with all your heart and with all your soul and with all your mind" (Matthew 22:37-38). In the pain of our lives we are built to turn to God in utter abandonment and to trust that His love will never fail us and that He will keep our souls safe until Homecoming. Our greatest sin is our unlove of God, our refusal to ground our lives in the soil of His love when we experience the disappointment of being let down by those closest to us.

God said to Jeremiah,

"My people have committed two sins:
They have forsaken me,
　　the spring of living water,

and have dug their own cisterns,
> broken cisterns that cannot hold water." (Jeremiah 2:13)

Like the Israelites of old, we have self-protectively looked for life in all the wrong places, trusting almost anything else but the One who alone can perfectly nourish and protect our lives. Our repentance must begin with confessing and abandoning our unlove toward God. It is only from this starting point that we can move into fulfilling the second greatest commandment: "Love your neighbor as yourself" (Matthew 22:39). We must first of all love and depend on God unreservedly, and then turn to those around us and treat them with love as well. Our fearful self-protection, however understandable, is a sinful violation of God's command—a violation for which we are without excuse.

LEGITIMATE REPENTING

My friend Marie is married to a Christian man who regularly beats her verbally and emotionally. Jim is to all external appearances the model husband, but when he loses his temper, he hurls incredibly destructive words at Marie. Her faults, her worthlessness, her intellectual incompetence, and her total inadequacy as a woman are his primary topics. Though she has no physical bruises or broken bones to "validate" the fact of her abuse, Jim's words leave her battered.

Most people (including the pastor she once spoke to in desperation) don't consider Marie an abused woman because there are no physical manifestations of her husband's cruelty. Yet the number of women in our churches who suffer terribly from their husbands' verbal and emotional beatings is growing every year. Like Marie, they live in either denial or continual fear. They carefully maintain their households and children in such a way as to prevent their husbands from becoming upset, believing they can thus assure themselves of kind treatment. Usually, this approach doesn't work.

Marie has tried several tactics in her attempts to change Jim's behavior. She has tried screaming back at him, matching cruel word for cruel word. She has tried speaking calmly to him about how he mistreats her (though when he accuses her of some misdemeanor or forgetfulness, blaming her for causing his tirade, she accepts the blame). So far, none of her tactics has curbed his abuse.

Jim's demeaning language (and the fact that his verbal battering occurs in front of their children and sometimes their guests) causes Marie great pain and anger. Yet when she considers Jesus' command to turn the other cheek, she feels guilty for these reactions. She thinks she is being "unsubmissive." Is she right to feel guilty? Should she confess her pain and anger to God as sin?

I think not. Marie's pain and anger are not sinful. They are normal, healthy, human responses to the enmity her husband so readily expresses to her. Her longing for esteem and protective cherishing from her husband is legitimate, and Jim's cruelty *should* provoke her pain and anger. Imbalance in God's world causes Him pain, too. Marie's sin is not in her desire that Jim be kind to her or in her pain when he fails to do so. Her yearning for Jim's protection and love is not the problem.

ACKNOWLEDGING THE SINFULNESS OF SELF-PROTECTION

The problem is that Marie, like all of us, is out to find a way to get her longings met somehow apart from God and to protect herself from being hurt—by her husband or anyone else.

This often happens in a marriage: Both partners come to the marriage with a legitimate longing to be seen and treated as worthwhile, adequate human beings in intimate relationship. But instead of husband and wife entering the union committed to finding love and enablement through their relationship with God and then giving out of personal fullness to meet each other's needs, each comes to marriage expecting to use the other person to get individual needs met.

The sin is not in the longing or the desire; the sin is in neglecting God's adequacy and in subconsciously intending to *use* instead of *love* the spouse. The partners have failed to love on both sides of the command. They do not love God by depending on Him, nor do they love their neighbor by being committed to meeting the other's needs. In their fallenness they are committed to getting their own needs met in their own way, rebelling against God's design for finding life in Him. Their theme is not "Have Thine Own Way, Lord," but "I Did It My Way."

The sin from which Marie must repent is a threefold failure. In her search for relief from pain, she is failing to trust God's love, to believe what God said about her, and to love Jim in the right way. Let's examine each failure and consider how she can appropriately repent.

Failure to Trust God's Love

Marie's self-sufficiency was her first failure. Instead of turning to the Father with her pain and trusting in His love as the bedrock of her inner life, she chose to protect herself from Jim's anger by working her strategies of control. She sinned when she was sweet to Jim so he wouldn't become upset. Her sweetness was motivated not by love but by fear of his mistreatment. She sinned by attempting to appease Jim when she accepted the blame for causing his verbal rampages. It was *his* choice, not hers, to act abusively toward her. Marie's apology for "making Jim angry" was every bit as wrong as her screaming cruelties at him, though it looked more "godly."

The motive of one's heart determines the morality of one's actions, and the motive for Marie's sweetness and apology was not trust in God's love to keep her from being destroyed on the inside; it was a desperate need to protect her inner self by staying out of Jim's way. Marie must repent not for her pain and anger, but for her belief that through her "submission" (i.e., acting submissive toward Jim while actually trying to control him) she could somehow manage her life. She must repent of her sweetness because it was a mask. Her submission did not flow out of trust and obedience to God. It stemmed from her need to change Jim, thus violating the very essence of true biblical submission, which is chosen yieldedness to her husband's legitimate need for respect.

This issue is complicated because Marie's actions appear normal and reasonable. We *expect* her to take things into her own hands because Jim's verbal abuse is so wrong. It's easy to identify with Marie because we have been in situations that caused us pain. We think it only reasonable to do what we must to either avoid the pain or interfere with what is causing it so we will no longer hurt. We know it is normal (and not sinful) to dislike pain, so we also think it is legitimate to make relief from pain our highest priority.

However, though our culture might disagree, it is *sinful* to avoid pain at any cost. According to Dr. Larry Crabb, people's real sin is not that they long for meaningful relationships, but that they

> *are moving in wrong directions in response to their thirst.* They refuse to trust God to look after their thirst. Instead, they insist on maintaining control of finding their own satisfaction. They're all moving about determined to satisfy the longings of their

hearts by picking up a shovel, looking for a likely spot to dig, and then searching for a fulfillment they can generate. To put it simply, people want to run their own lives. Fallen man is both terrified of vulnerability and committed to maintaining independence.[2]

God calls us to turn to Him in our pain and admit we cannot sustain our inner lives. He alone is life, and our pain is purposeful—God's own custom pain job to bring us to utter dependence on His love toward us. This is not to say that Marie should allow the abuse to continue and simply pray to feel more loved by God. The primary question Marie must ask if she truly repents is this: In what way am I failing to believe in God's lovingkindness toward me when my priority is to protect myself from pain? As long as her purpose in life is to stay out of pain (rather than to rely on God's truth about her value and to learn to love others), she will not repent of her self-protective strategies or be able to love Jim correctly. She must repent by changing her purpose from self-protection to risking Jim's rejection, made possible only through a deeper faith in God's sustaining love.

Failure to Believe What God Said about Her
Marie's second failure flows out of and is closely related to her first. A deep part of her unbelief in God's love for her is her unwillingness to believe in her value. Most women who allow themselves to continue in an abusive relationship (physical, verbal, sexual, or emotional) do so because they cherish a negative image of themselves. Believing they deserve the mistreatment they regularly receive, many feel more comfortable (i.e. natural) being abused than being affirmed in a relationship.

Negating one's value may look submissive and sound humble, but Marie actually chooses to believe and act on a lie. The lie says that she is unworthy of being loved or esteemed; therefore, anything cruel Jim might say or do is a legitimate reflection of her worthlessness. Her belief in that lie is a sin from which she must repent.

The truth that Marie should believe and act on is that God places an incredibly high value on her. She is His precious child, uniquely fashioned by Him before her very birth (Psalm 139:13-18) and so loved by Him that He laid down His life for her (John 3:16). If she is thus esteemed by the God of the universe through His creation and redemption of her, she sins when she refuses to place that same value on herself. It is like being offered a million dollars and shouting in the benefactor's face, "I won't take your money! I'm a poor woman, and I won't let you rob me of my poverty!"

For years, what Marie considered meekness in the face of adversity was actually self-contempt, utterly dishonorable to the God in whose image she is made. Every time she allows herself to be abused by her husband, she calls God a liar. In effect she says that His creation and redemption of her count for less than her efforts at self-denial.

Unless Marie repents of her disbelief and begins to act as though Jim's verbal abuse is an affront to the integrity of God's Word about her worth, she will remain in her sin and allow both herself and her marriage to be destroyed unnecessarily. On the other hand, if she repents and confronts Jim's abuse by speaking the truth about her true value before the Father, Jim's anger (and verbal battering) will likely increase. She will wonder whether God meant for her to remain in her abusive situation indefinitely. The real question, however, is not *whether* but *how* Marie is to go on with Jim. If she will face her pain and learn to cry out to the Father in the midst of her unhappy circumstances (He never asks us to be anywhere but at the end of ourselves), she will find in His daily affirmation of her the strength she needs to disbelieve Jim's lies (verbal and behavioral) about her lack of value.

Marie's recovery from her sinful self-contempt will take considerable time and will probably require the assistance of other Christians who will pray for her and affirm God's true opinion of her. Many abused women also find helpful (even necessary) some kind of involvement in counseling and/or a recovery group to learn why they choose to continually revictimize themselves. That understanding, combined with ongoing repentance for their unbelief and a willingness to face their pain, will enable them to gradually break out of their self-bondage to abuse and change both their thinking and their acting.

Even though Jim may not change his abusive behavior right away (perhaps not at all), Marie can learn to stop accepting his negative statements about her worth and, on the basis of God's cherishing of her, take the steps necessary to refuse his abuse. In that way Jim's abusive words will gradually lose their power to destroy her on the inside. If Marie will genuinely repent of her sin of disbelieving God's valuing of her, over time the destructive pattern of verbal abuse in her marriage can be broken.

Failure to Love the Right Way

The third sin for which Marie must repent is her failure to love Jim the right way. Because she is consumed with keeping herself safe from his verbal battering, she is unable to love him with the dignity and respect he needs from her. He doesn't need her to apologize for making him angry; he needs her to say his anger is not a valid reason for his abusive behavior. He doesn't need her sweetness when he is badgering her; he needs her to declare with conviction, "I don't deserve this kind of treatment. I am not all those things you are saying I am. I am a valued and loved child of the King of the universe, and you may not speak to me like that!"

Marie shows profound disrespect for both Jim and herself when she lets him go on sinning against her. She must refuse to receive the battering, perhaps by leaving the room or even the house during his attack, especially when guests are present, with an explanation of what she is doing and why. It will surely take time for her to build up the courage to take that kind of step. But as Marie lives out her repentance for not believing in her worth, she will by those very actions also learn to love Jim the right way, showing him the respect of honest confrontation and open involvement with the "real Marie."

Furthermore, if Jim is battering the children, Marie is responsible to speak up on their behalf because they are beloved and valued by the Father. She must protect them from the terrible damage being done to their self-esteem. Again, the process will not be easy and it will take time to undo the patterns of abuse and victimization, but real hope is available for those who will repent of their sinful self-protection and self-contempt by learning to live step by step a new way.

What about women who are physically abused by their husbands? Must they yield to violence as an expression of "submission"? In her excellent book about domestic violence toward women, *In the Name of Submission*, Kay Marshall-Storm rightly insists that wife-battering (which is a discouragingly frequent problem in the Christian Church) should never be accommodated as an acceptable expression of a husband's authority over his wife. God never intended a husband's authority to be used by him to control, hurt, or punish an "unsubmissive" wife; rather, he is to pour out his life for her with *agape* love. If he abdicates that responsibility and beats his wife and children, his sin must be named and challenged. In fact, his wife is being unloving toward herself, her children, *and her husband* when she remains willing to ignore and perpetuate his sin.

When Abigail found her entire household threatened with disaster because of her husband's sin, she did what she could to secure safety for them, yet did not violate her commitment to her marriage or manipulate her husband, Nabal. (See 1 Samuel 25.) A woman whose physical safety (and that of her children) is in danger has a responsibility to keep her husband from sinning against them further, by calling the authorities for protection or by physically removing herself and her children from jeopardy. She must then seek the help (particularly long-term professional help) she and her husband need to change their deeply ingrained patterns. Protecting oneself from physical harm is not sinful, but it must be done in the context of commitment to the marriage (if it is salvageable) and to personal growth spiritually and emotionally.

OBSTACLES TO REPENTANCE

One of the great inhibitors of true repentance is stubborn self-sufficiency. We are men and women who would be kings and queens of our own lives, finding life in people or pleasure, accomplishments or ministry, rather than in Christ. It is not that we intellectually disagree with Jesus that life is to be found in Him alone. It is just that we do not live that way.

We have made our declaration of independence from God, leaning on our strategies for meeting our desperate need for affirmation and safety. I am committed to making Bill into the strong, loving man I need so I'll never have to fear abandonment or rejection. He is equally committed to changing me into his mental image of a submissive, charming wife who will never let him down or expose his inadequacies. This seems somehow so much more down-to-earth than trusting God for our inner lives.

Despite the fact that the Father calls us to walk in the dark, trusting in His Word and relying on His leading through the Holy Spirit, we have lit our torches so that we can see for ourselves the path ahead. God's judgment on us is this: "You will lie down in torment" (Isaiah 50:10-11). He has called us to love Him above all else, but we have put our safety first. My fear that Bill will leave me emotionally runs much deeper than my faith that God will sustain me even if that happens. Bill's anxiety about my disrespect and abandonment motivates his actions far more than does his trust in God's presence (regardless of my opinion of him).

Before we can repent of our sinful strategies of self-protective unlove toward our spouses, we must acknowledge that our self-sufficiency is the root sin demanding our repentance. It will be impossible to truly repent of our failure over the second commandment (to love others as ourselves) unless we first repent of our failure over the first (to love and trust God above all else). We must abandon ourselves utterly to the Father and acknowledge on a daily basis that spiritual life is found only in Him.

A second obstacle to true repentance is our sense of having been injured out of proportion to what we have done wrong. Our spouses' sins against us both dwarf and somehow justify our sin of self-protection. Sometimes the injury has been so severe that we push self-protection all the way to revenge. I know a woman for whom avenging her pain became an obsession. In a moment of honest insight she admitted she did not want to repent and she did not want her husband to repent, because then she would have to forgive him and she wanted him to suffer for what he had done to her over the years.

I understand. It's always easier for me to recognize someone else's sin against me than to admit my own. Nevertheless, it is our self-protection (including the safe-seeking of vengeance) that God has called us to acknowledge and name and from which we must turn in repentance. We must admit that however we may try to justify it, our hidden agenda has been not to love but to be loved, which violates God's perfect law. I have often demanded that Bill come through for me before I offer my forgiveness and love—and God calls that sin. We must overcome the revenge-seeking obstacle to inner repentance by facing our deep commitment to sinful self-protection.

Another obstacle to repentance is our natural abhorrence of exposure. We hate to face our failure at loving, and even more than that, we hate to have others recognize we have failed. Our self-protective unlove goes beyond the obvious sinful choices we make, such as refusing to be honest about our lives, taking blame when we shouldn't, avoiding conflict, hiding behind a jovial facade, maintaining control in our relationships, and so on. The exposure we fear most is the realization that our very nature makes us incapable of loving others in the right way. It is not just what we do but who we are that we hate to acknowledge, even to ourselves. It is excruciating to move from wondering, *How can I be that bad?* to admitting, *That is how bad I am.*

We want to believe that we'll find life if we can just get rid of the pain; so we refuse to accept God's diagnosis of the seriousness of our problem. We prefer more acceptable explanations: We have a poor self-image, we're just bossy by nature, we can't be blamed for not loving others when they're being thoughtless, or we inherited our temper from our parents. The list is endless.

Refusing to examine our innate self-centeredness, we remain committed to changing our circumstances, intent on winning our spouses' love or approval or respect or tenderness or strength (whatever we need that is being withheld). We fail to distinguish between the legitimate *desire* that our spouses change and the illegitimate *demand* (of them and of God) that they become what we need. And as long as our spirits *demand* the change, we are idolaters, worshiping anxiously at the shrine of our mates' acceptance and approval instead of kneeling thankfully at the foot of the cross where Jesus proved His love to us beyond the shadow of a doubt. Our self-diagnosis is that we have only a minor problem; our self-prognosis is that it is curable by our efforts; and our self-treatment is to redouble our efforts to get others to change so that we won't be in so much pain.

Jeremiah has reminded us that our hearts are "deceitful above all things, and desperately wicked" (Jeremiah 17:9, KJV). Without Jesus, we cannot love at all, and even with His Spirit indwelling us, we struggle with a nature that insistently drives us to self-protection. We must be willing to admit this deep-rooted propensity to utterly selfish living if we are to know the joyous release of true repentance and forgiveness.

NEW PURPOSES

Repentance, then, involves two things: recognizing the sinful purpose of our lives (to stay out of pain by protecting ourselves in any way we can) and embracing a new purpose (to utterly trust God for our inner lives by dropping our self-protection and moving with openness toward our mates according to their legitimate needs). This we must do without making excuses for our failure to love. Before God, there is no excuse for breaking His commandments.

There is also no accommodation for penance as we face the sin of self-protection. The purpose of self-protection, in fact, is the same as the purpose of penance—to stay in control by substituting some positive external behavior instead of becoming genuinely open in the relationship. A spouse who is committed to "doing better next time" may simply be resorting to a new strategy for protecting himself or herself from future failure. Genuine repentance admits the deep and sinful nature of our devoted commitment to self-sufficiency and, thus, does not rely on future performance to make up for the sinful self-protection of the past. We must acknowledge with unflinching candor the misdirected purposes and stubborn rootedness of our strategies for staying safe in our marriage relationships.

Our candor pleases the Father. Confession always does. We give Him glory when we declare He is right in naming and condemning our sin. Joshua, for example, instructed thieving Achan to confess, saying, "My son, give glory to the LORD, the God of Israel, and give him the praise. Tell me what you have done; do not hide it from me" (Joshua 7:19). And David's prayer of confession regarding his sin with Bathsheba included these words to God:

Against you, you only, have I sinned
    and done what is evil in your sight,
so that you are proved right when you speak
    and justified when you judge. (Psalm 51:4)

Confession glorifies God by declaring both His holiness and His justice in condemning our sin.

But more than justifying God in His accurate naming of our sin, our repentance and honest confession open the way to our complete cleansing from sin and restoration of fellowship with God. The Apostle John summed it up this way: "If we claim to be without sin, we deceive ourselves and the truth is not in us. If we confess our sins, he is faithful and just and will forgive us our sins and purify us from all unrighteousness" (1 John 1:8-9).

As we practice ongoing repentance of our self-protective strategies, we can walk clean into a new day every day with our spouses. Grace through the blood of Jesus will become a reality we live by, not merely a doctrine we hold to, and old sins will lose their long-held power over us.

In the following chapters we will consider the specifics of living out our repentance, and we will discover that what God calls us to as we change in our intimate relationships isn't going to be easy. But those who have experienced the exhilaration of being forgiven afresh at every recognition and acknowledgment of their sin know that the pain of confession is infinitely worth the gain of inner restfulness. Nothing can compare to living by grace, cleansed continually by the blood of the Lamb!

When we acknowledge the sinfulness of our behavior and our intentions to stay safe and we find the promised cleansing, repentance then demands that we turn from our old strategies and intend a new thing. We must commit ourselves to dispelling our fear by dropping our self-protection. Repentance calls us to sacrifice our former fearful behaviors and change our minds about what life is all about. We must purpose not to play it safe, but to live increasingly without self-protection in our marriages, trusting in God alone to protect our inner lives from disaster. That is what it means to genuinely repent.

PURSUING REPENTANCE

Repentance must be genuine; cheap repentance carries no power. A person who bypasses the soul-wrenching recognition of his or her desperate bentness toward sin (characterized by the failure to love) may make external behavioral changes, but those changes will not survive the test of time. Nor is there to be just a one-time repentance. Sorrow and confession must happen every time we see our sin of unlove repeat itself in a new form; it is the only way we can hope for spiritual maturing and significant change in our marriages.

One of the hallmarks of true repentance is that those who practice it continue to pursue it, even when it may not "work" to change things in the marriage. Often when we repent, we do so with the expectation that our increased spirituality will convince our partners that they, too, should repent and change. Despite the other's refusal to change, genuine repentance perseveres, and instead of being discouraged by the discovery of new evidence of self-protection, the person who truly repents becomes eager to learn how he or she is self-protecting in order to learn how to become a better lover.

Though believers will probably never fully lose their dread of seeing their unlove exposed, they can come to welcome the Spirit's convicting as another opportunity for cleansing and for learning to love as Jesus loved. Instead of running from conviction, they will face and grievingly acknowledge the radical bentness of their self-seeking nature whenever He shows it to them. Their hearts will be open to the loving rebuke of fellow believers, agreeing with the proverbs that state, "The kisses of an enemy may be profuse, but faithful are the wounds of a friend" (Proverbs 27:6, NIV 1978 version), and "He who listens to a life-giving rebuke will be at home among the wise" (Proverbs 15:31).

The natural man's reaction to being shown his faults is resentment, denial, or self-defense, but those whose lives are exercised by godly repentance actively seek to know how they are not being loving in a certain circumstance so they can repent, receive God's grace through Christ, and choose to change.

This kind of repentance is possible only to those who know what it means to live by grace, forgiven of sins of unlove by the boundless mercy of God because of Jesus' death on the cross. By the same token, this kind of repentance is required of those who are so forgiven and so loved. If we will receive the love and forgiveness of God, we must also repent of our self-protection and move into genuine openness in our relationships with others as well, especially our marriage partners.

SUMMING UP

Repentance is essentially an internal exercise, a change of mind or purpose that happens in our hearts. But God also calls us to live out our repentance behaviorally, excising from our lives by the power of the Holy Spirit the old self-protective habits of living for our spouses' approval or of controlling others so they will meet our needs.

When John the Baptist called the Jews of his day to repent because God's Kingdom was at hand, he added this requirement: "Produce fruit in keeping with repentance" (Matthew 3:8). The instructions he then gave to Jewish citizens, tax collectors, and soldiers described actions that would give evidence of their repentance from their former sin.

It is so with us as well. If John were here, he would say the same thing to us: "Produce fruit in keeping with repentance." When we repent of our sinful self-protection and lack of love, certain behaviors will appear in our lives that will reveal to us and others the genuine repentance of our hearts. The next section will explore the process of living out repentance in our marriages as husbands seek to sacrificially love their wives and as wives begin to understand and develop a biblically submissive attitude toward their husbands.

NOTES:
1. W.E. Vine, "repent," *Vine's Expository Dictionary of Old and New Testament Words,* vol. 3 (Old Tappan, N.J.: Fleming H. Revell, 1981), page 280.
2. Larry Crabb, *Inside Out* (Colorado Springs, Colo.: NavPress, 1988), page 54.

QUESTIONS FOR THOUGHT AND DISCUSSION

1. List several things you legitimately long for from your marriage partner (present or future).

2. Use an example from a marriage you know well to explain the difference between legitimate longings and sinful self-protection.

3. How does your particular style of self-protection violate the first and greatest command to love God with all that you are?

4. In what ways does your self-protection violate the second commandment to love others as yourself, particularly in your marriage?

5. Give two specific examples of how you can become vulnerable in a good way (facing your inner fears) in your relationship with your spouse or an intimate friend.

6. Why would it be necessary for someone to repent of being sweet and kind in a marriage relationship?

3

CHOICE:
Dropping the Masks

9

CLIFF-JUMPING:
Taking Risks

In the first section of this book, we explored several masks of submission behind which many women live so that they can protect themselves from the pain of what is really going on beneath the surface of their marriages. We saw how both husbands and wives use their roles of authority or submission to hide their underlying fear of rejection and failure. The result is often an emptiness and pain in the very covenantal relationships that should afford them the greatest blessing.

The second section described the legitimate needs of husbands and wives as created image-bearers of God and illustrated how God intended for those needs to be met according to His design for marriage. We examined how our fallenness has caused us to disobey God's command to love Him above all and our neighbor (spouse) as ourselves. Our disobedience is that we have become self-sufficient (turning from God to pursue our own ways of finding life), self-protective (hiding from God and from each other), and self-seeking (using each other to get our needs met). God calls us to repent of this triple sin of unlove.

If we truly repent from the heart, it will show. And the most telling evidence of true repentance in a marriage partner is the willingness to do whatever is the loving thing for the other, dropping the mask of self-protection. When one partner is willing to admit personal sin and minister genuinely to the other, true repentance is at work, and real change is possible. But not without risk.

TAKING RISKS

Repentance and love always involve risk. The lengths to which I will go to keep myself personally safe never cease to amaze me. My fear of rejection and disapproval runs so deep that almost any physical danger is preferable to facing my inner terror. The patterns of relating we develop for protecting ourselves are varied and subtle, but the goal is always the same: finding and keeping a safe place for ourselves. However, we cannot operate out of fear and faith at the same time. When we are afraid, we cancel out our trust in God (or anyone else). We cannot be equally committed to trusting God and to playing it safe with our spouses. We have to choose.

Recall the relationship between Tom and Lorraine discussed in chapter 2. Their marriage was built on fear and dedicated to mutual safety, not risk. Lorraine hated to make choices, and allowing Tom to be the decision-maker permitted her to avoid her fear of failure, a fear dating back to her relationship with a distant and disapproving father. Lorraine backed away from displeasing Tom not because she trusted his leadership, but because she was terrified of his disapproval. Depending on him for her identity, she had to be acceptable to him, or she could not find herself acceptable. Letting Tom know how she really felt (about him, about their marriage, about how he treated the children) was unthinkable. He might give her that look of disdain or condescension she so dreaded—what she called (to herself) his look of death. To save herself from the shame of his look, she denied her true self. It was not love that motivated Lorraine's submission; she simply would not risk the pain.

Tom was afraid, too. His need to stay in charge was rooted in his fear of inadequacy. He could not allow Lorraine to challenge him because he could not admit he was wrong about anything. His military training reinforced his belief that failure meant death, and in his home life that belief worked itself out in a decisive, aggressive leadership style that did nothing to satisfy the emotional needs of his family.

Behind his facade of strength lay deep insecurity. Lorraine's dream of becoming a teacher threatened him because a career would lessen her dependence on him, especially financially, and he would lose the control her dependence provided him as well as the superficial sense of adequacy he enjoyed from her nonassertiveness.

Tom and Lorraine's dependence on each other had not been the healthy interdependence of two redeemed image-bearers; it was a mutual demand that the other fulfill needs that had gone unmet in the past. Openness with each other was not an option because it meant risking what felt like personal death (i.e., the other person's rejection). In fact, their strategies of self-protection were causing a mutual resentment that was slowly killing their marriage from the inside. A proverb illuminates their problem: "There is a way that seems right to a man, but in the end it leads to death" (Proverbs 14:12). Neither Tom nor Lorraine was trusting God or doing the loving thing for the other. Committed to staying safe, they could neither trust nor risk.

Tom and Lorraine's hope for genuine life in their relationship depends on their willingness to abandon their masks of protection, trust God for His utterly dependable love, and risk loving each other without demandingness. Jesus said, "Whoever wants to save his life will lose it, but whoever loses his life for me will find it" (Matthew 16:25). Life is to be found by letting go of whatever it is in our marriage relationship that we fear we cannot live without and by embracing Jesus as our only source of life. What a risk!

JUMPING FROM CLIFFS

Taking risks means doing whatever moves a marriage partner away from particular self-protective strategies and toward ministering love to the other partner (according to the individual need for respect and love). In *The Marriage-Builder*, Dr. Larry Crabb compares risk-taking in marriage to jumping off a cliff.[1] He pictures the wife in his illustration standing on what he calls a cliff of safety overlooking an abyss of rejection. Tied around her waist is a limp-lying rope of love attached upward to the strong hand of God, invisible above the abyss. If the illustration is applied to marriage, the action this wife must take is to jump off her cliff of safety (i.e., abandon her self-protective strategy of control) into the abyss of her husband's possible rejection (i.e., act toward him with risky, no-strings-attached respect and trust), believing that God's love will keep her from being destroyed on the rocks of rejection below. A husband's cliff-jumping would follow the same procedure, though the strategies he abandons would differ from hers, as would the ways he involves himself strongly and lovingly in her life.

When one or both spouses jump from their cliffs of safety, it is likely they will experience profound personal pain while they wait to experience God's sufficiency. What they most fear in terms of relational disappointment might very well happen. But personal pain is not the same as personal destruction, though both feel like death.

God's men and women in Scripture were "purified" by suffering as they became truly useful to God. Joseph was enslaved, Moses lost everything, Hannah grieved both to conceive and later to surrender Samuel, David became a fugitive, Abigail was married to a fool, and Paul endured innumerable persecutions. Their pain, though terrible, strengthened them as they yielded to God's purpose and leaned on His presence in the process. A husband's or wife's cliff-jumping will be painful, but it will not destroy. Rather, it will produce an increasingly radiant living by grace as it puts the person into a new, even desperate, dependence on God's love.

My process of marital cliff-jumping was terrifying. I had always affirmed that God's sovereign love would undergird me through any possible calamity, but I took great care to maintain my circumstances so I wouldn't have to test it out. Then came the day several years ago when I asked God to bring revival into my life, and He began by casting me into a period of spiritual depression I thought I wouldn't survive.

During that time, I blamed Bill and my church leaders and my friends for my desert experience. (Why weren't they meeting my spiritual needs!?) I didn't realize God was in the process of salting my thirst for Him until I longed for His presence more than for life itself. I lacked the audacity of Moses asking to see God's face; the burning bush would do. And as I began to see the Father manifested in my wilderness, I also heard Him calling me to confront some previously ignored realities in my life, particularly about my relationship with Bill.

Gradually, I had to face my disappointments and fears, my dishonesty with Bill about my true feelings, and my self-protective withholding of my inner self while demanding (in very sweet ways, of course) that Bill be for me what I needed him to be. When I began to risk honesty with Bill about those inner realities, our marriage started coming apart at the seams, and the leap from my cliff of safety sent me plummeting toward what felt like certain death. Never had I known such fear, but neither had I ever experienced so powerfully the reality and constancy of God's presence. His rope of love sustained me.

During my years of process since then, God's sovereignty has sometimes been all I've had to hang on to. If I hadn't known He was in charge for my good, my life would not have been worth living. Though often my relationship with Bill caused as much pain as I'd always feared it might (and sometimes more), I found God to be enough.

As Christian spouses, most of us believe God loves us unconditionally and equips us for adequacy, but when our mates do not love or respect us, when the marriage is on rocky ground and we feel the disappointment of our partners' unlove, the reality of our security is thrown into question. It's hard to believe in God's love when we're not *feeling* loved by our marriage partners. Cliff-jumping means giving up the "security" of trying to make our partners be more loving. Instead we are to trust God to be true to His Word that He unconditionally loves us, even when we do not experience such love with each other.

Few of us have allowed ourselves to get that desperate for the presence and love of God. We would much rather seek life in those things over which we can exercise some degree of control—our careers, our children, our gifts, our spouses, our ministries—whatever works to make us feel good. Yet in our honest moments we must confess that if we have managed to stay relatively safe, we also have failed to genuinely experience the abundant spiritual life Jesus promised in John 10:10.

Perhaps we are drawn toward a few "saints" we know or have read about who possess the inner strength and tranquility that flow from abandonment and intimacy with God, but most of us aren't distinguished by those attributes with any consistency. I suspect it is because we are unwilling to be stripped down (as they undoubtedly were) to needing God for our very survival. Surely the risks we are called to take as we live out our repentance for self-protection in our marriages are substantial, but I have experienced firsthand that aliveness in God is worth the cost. Leaving my safe places felt like death, but I was thrown into the exhilarating life of raw, desperate faith. I entered into what my sister calls the terror of grace.

Taking personal risks is always accompanied by a profound fear of the pain of being rejected by the one we most want to love us. The sad truth is that our worst fears will undoubtedly be realized simply because all marriage partners are fallen human beings and cannot help but let each other down, especially when what is happening in the marriage is unexpected. Change is always painful. The tragedy is that most spouses would rather avoid the possibility of pain (the partner's rejection or disrespect) than risk discovering God's sufficiency to carry them beyond the pain to genuine, supernatural love for each other. As the saying goes, "No pain, no gain."

A WORD OF CAUTION

Christ is indeed sufficient to meet our need for love and adequacy, but His sufficiency should never become a substitute for one spouse's involvement with the other. At one point in my process I thought that because Christ is the perfect Lover, I shouldn't have to depend on Bill, and so I could emotionally walk away from him. Just the opposite is true.

Paul taught that "woman is not independent of man, nor is man independent of woman" (1 Corinthians 11:11). God designed marriage so that a wife *should* depend on her husband to minister to her need for love and esteem as God ordained (even when he doesn't do it perfectly); his gift to her is to cherish and love her so that she will *feel* the love God Himself has for her. And a husband *should* desire his wife to respond to his leadership with trust and respect as God ordained (even though she's not perfect, either); her gift to him is to affirm his adequacy by her willingness to risk depending on him.

They should lean on each other with the realization that, because they are human, they will at some point let each other down and will feel the pain and disappointment of rejection and inadequacy. At that point each spouse must give up the goal of changing the other (trying to not be let down again), and instead look to the Father as the only unconditional Lover of his or her life. Then they must move again toward each other in God's strength to be the best lovers they can be, offering each other their honesty, their need, their respect, and their love from the heart. God intended His love to be the undergirding *support* but not a *substitute* for the mutual dependence of marriage partners.

LIVING IN THE TERROR OF GRACE

What is involved in cliff-jumping? What exactly must a person do who wants to genuinely take personal risk in his or her marriage and learn to trust God by unconditionally loving his or her mate? The next two chapters will attempt to answer that question in greater detail, but the rule of thumb for knowing how to risk is this: Consider doing whatever is hardest to do. Whatever generates the most fear (because it threatens the most inner pain) is usually exactly what we ought to do or at least be willing to do. It is probably the area where we most jealously protect ourselves and most seriously miss loving our mates. In precisely those areas we must practice dropping our self-protective masks and risk making the changes that will move us toward loving with openness and abandon.

For example, Kerri, the middle-aged woman whose story is told in chapter 1, faced one of her deepest fears when she was willing to consider the possibility that her husband, Steve, might be an alcoholic like her father. The risk she took in attending weekly meetings for the families of substance abusers was substantial. Even the thought of reminding Steve that she would be going to her meeting Tuesday night caused terrible knots of fear in her stomach. And her fears were justified. When she did remind him, Steve's anger and the fallout of that anger for her and their children made his rejection a painful reality. Yet throughout their Terrible Year, Kerri's fear for her inner safety was her clue as to what risks she ought to take in her relationship with Steve.

Kerri was able to face those risks only because of God's sustaining love. In the midst of her pain at Steve's turning from her, Kerri fled in desperation to the Father just to emotionally survive their family turmoil. Moreover, she kept on risking, continuing to confront Steve's drinking pattern. She knew that if she could make changes in her wrong patterns of protecting him and enabling him in his drinking, then Steve might also be willing to face and deal with his problem and its causes. Her greatest risk was that Steve might leave her and abandon the marriage rather than face himself. But she discovered that God would never forsake or leave her without His guiding presence, no matter what happened with the marriage. Kerri was learning to live a day at a time in the terror of grace.

FACING THE PAIN

Dropping self-protective masks in an intimate relationship is never easy or painless. Someone is bound to get hurt. That is why so few people are willing to get the help they need to change their destructive patterns of relating, and that is also why so few marriages evidence the genuine love and mutual respect God intended them to have.

I felt discouraged not long ago when someone asked how many marriages I knew were healthy and growing. I could name only a few, which is a regrettable evaluation to have to make. If the goal is to stay out of pain (or to get out of the pain they are already in), people will never risk making the changes that can move them toward becoming better lovers, and several things will be true of their lives.

First, they will have little rich experience of God's love and grace in life. Maintaining the status quo and refusing to look inside are exactly what the Pharisees did, who opposed Jesus during His earthly ministry. They so concentrated on polishing the exteriors of their lives that they failed to see their inner filth from which Jesus could have cleansed them. Jesus dealt more harshly with their sin of hypocrisy than with such gross immorality as thievery and adultery. Grace cannot flourish—perhaps cannot even survive—when individuals will not risk looking honestly at their sinful patterns and seek God's help to forgive and change. Risk is absolutely essential to spiritual growth and vitality.

Moreover, a marriage in which the partners refuse to risk changing will ultimately offer only an illusion of intimacy, each individual relating only from personal layers of self-protection. In such a marriage there will be little real touching of each other on the deep levels of legitimate need, little reciprocal love and esteem, little true submission to genuine godly authority. A surface relationship—mere coping with the circumstances of life—is all the partners in a no-risk marriage will have to look forward to. Both will miss out on the excitement of living by grace, making mistakes, and learning to forgive and be forgiven in an ever-growing relationship with God and with each other. What a waste!

There is another danger involved in living without risk. People who refuse to change and instead choose to live with unresolved anger and pain in any relationship will end up being worn down (physically and emotionally), or they will eventually look for a way to escape. Marriage partners who refuse to look inside and change what needs to be changed may become bitter or abusive toward their mates, blaming them for their own unhappiness. Or they may find illicit ways to dull their frustration and boredom. Addiction to alcohol and drugs is on the increase, even among Christians. So are workaholism and the incidence of extramarital affairs. Needs do not go away when they are ignored. They merely go underground. When thirsty people refuse to repent of their respectable but futile well-digging and turn to the Fountain of living water, they often end up digging remarkably unrespectable wells to try to quench their thirst.

One final consideration: When one person in a marriage is willing to change and grow but the other is not, the risk for the relationship is substantial. In some cases the marriage will be jeopardized by the spiritual revival of one partner. This dilemma will be discussed in greater detail in a later chapter, but here it needs to be said that when a man or woman begins to walk in obedience to God's call to personal revival, the Holy Spirit will bring such joy and newness of life that everything will be rearranged (2 Corinthians 5:17).

Disruption in the marriage is to be expected, but as with all God-ordained disruption, it will over time result in inner tranquility for those whose lives continue to be exercised by the Holy Spirit. Sometimes the aliveness of soul that comes from walking God's narrow road is all a marriage partner will have to cling to in the lonely pilgrimage toward living married and unmasked, but that aliveness is worth the cost of discipleship. The one who risks all for the sake of Christ's fellowship will never regret the exchange.

SUMMING UP

There are no easy solutions to the problems that face us in our marriages, and there are no ultimately safe places where we can avoid the reality of our own sin and the sinfulness of others. God left His people in a world of pressure and temptation and suffering, but He told us not to be of the world. People "of the world" must play it safe in their marriages because no safety net of God's love is beneath them.

But believers in Jesus can begin moving one day at a time and one step at a time away from self-protection and toward greater honesty and less demandingness in their marriages. Freedom will not happen all at once, and we will find ourselves seeking safe harbor in our old habits again and again. Yet God persistently calls us to renewed risk-taking and assures us of His unfailing love and sure presence in the midst of any circumstance. To be alive in Him is to be willing to risk. Particularly in our marriages we are called to cliff-jumping and other calisthenics, which the next chapters will examine.

NOTE:
1. Lawrence J. Crabb, Jr., *The Marriage Builder* (Grand Rapids: Zondervan Publishing House, 1986), pages 38-41.

QUESTIONS FOR THOUGHT AND DISCUSSION

1. In your intimate relationships what most feels like death when you think of doing it?

2. How do you avoid or protect yourself from that?

3. Identify the risk you might take if you genuinely repented of your self-protection in that area.

4. Read about each of the following Old Testament heroes of faith (listed in Hebrews 11). What risks did they take that evidenced repentance for not trusting God and/or for not genuinely loving others?
•Noah (Genesis 6)
•Abraham (Genesis 12:1-4)
•Moses (Exodus 3)
•Rahab (Joshua 2)

5. Name at least one thing you can do in your marriage that would be a cliff-jumping calisthenic for you.

6. What are some benefits of jumping from your cliff of safety in your intimate relationship?

10

CLOAK-SHEDDING:
Speaking the Truth

Cliff-jumping (taking personal risks of repentance and change instead of playing it safe with one's marriage partner) is a necessary calisthenic for developing a healthy marriage. It involves two particular exercises: telling the truth and letting go of control. This chapter deals with the first exercise, telling the truth in love.

Facing the truth is not a simple task. For one thing, we do not always know the truth, particularly the truth about ourselves. I can remember my mid-life trauma of realizing I did not know who I was because I'd spent my life being all things to all people. When people asked what I liked or wanted, I really didn't know. I could not have told them the truth about myself because I did not know the "real me."

Being honest is also uncomfortable. We dread removing the familiar masks to examine our longings or to tell others (particularly our spouses) who we really are. That untruthfulness comes not from our inability to express ourselves clearly but from our unwillingness to look at ourselves honestly. Having inherited from our first parents a stubborn habit of connecting nakedness (i.e., genuine honesty) with shame, we have become what R.C. Sproul calls "fugitives from [God's] gaze" as well as strangers to our spouses' gaze. We identify with

Sproul's description of Adam and Eve: "They wanted their nakedness and their shame hidden, yet yearned for a safe place to be naked. They yearned for a place where they could take off their clothes and be known without fear. God provided that place in the institution of marriage."[1] Yet even in our marriages, we hide our true feelings behind a facade of acceptable talk and refuse to look at the deep loneliness we experience as a result of the hiding. Our masks have so concealed us that the real person inside can't be known.

RUNNING FROM THE TRUTH

Why are we so reluctant to tell the truth? What keeps us in bondage to the lies of our lives? Sometimes we're afraid to be honest because we hate to face the pain our self-protective strategies are designed to avoid. Who wants to reopen old wounds or irritate fresh ones? Also, we dislike hurting our mates' feelings, not always because we care about them so much but because we fear they can't handle hearing the truth and therefore need our protection (an evidence of our disrespect, not love). Or we may refuse to speak up because we don't trust our perceptions of reality; thinking ourselves worthless, we mistrust the validity of our ideas.

Perhaps our deepest reason for not revealing our true selves is that we are afraid of being rejected. What if we tell who we are or say what we feel, and our partners turn away? The fear runs deep, and honesty exposes us to the possibility of experiencing what we most dread. The risks of truth-telling are substantial.

Why, then, risk telling the truth at all? Why not just leave well enough alone and keep our masks of dishonesty safely in place? Part of the answer, of course, is that God commands it. Paul instructed the Ephesian Christians to "put off falsehood and speak truthfully" (Ephesians 4:25). If honesty is a hallmark of renewed living in Christ's Church, how much more so should Christian marriages reflect that same openness?

But beyond the obedience issue, truth-telling in marriage is also an integrity issue. Spouses who drop their masks and risk becoming "real" increase the likelihood of intimacy with each other; one cannot have intimacy with a stranger. A marriage built on pretense is a mere shell, both partners playing hide-and-seek and never finding one another. If a marriage is to do more than just survive, if it is to thrive, each partner must be willing to risk being deeply honest with—and possibly deeply hurt by—the other.

AVOIDING EXTREMES

How should we tell ourselves and our partners the truth? Should we just say anything and everything that comes into our minds? Are there guidelines to help us know what truth-telling we should do and when?

Surely we should avoid the two extremes. Some people simply stuff their true feelings and refuse to acknowledge even to themselves how a hurtful remark or action affected them. Stuffing as a lifestyle takes enormous effort and causes significant internal tension. The short-term benefits (avoidance of conflict) are almost always outweighed by the destructive, sometimes explosive, long-term physical and emotional consequences.

Other people dump their feelings and say exactly how they feel, when they feel it, to whoever is closest or most responsible for the pain. Dumping feels good to the dumper, but the dumpee pays a high price, emotionally and sometimes physically. Both stuffing and dumping are unbiblical and unhealthy ways to deal with pain.

TELLING THE TRUTH

Paul instructed all Christians: "Do not let any unwholesome talk come out of your mouths, but only what is helpful for building others up according to their needs, that it may benefit those who listen" (Ephesians 4:29). But how can we tell the truth to each other in ways that will build up rather than tear down? What should be the subject of our truth-telling?

There are two aspects of our lives about which we must speak the truth in love: our pain and our sin. We must be willing to face our deep yearnings for love (which will cause us pain because those longings cannot be fulfilled in this life) and our wrong strategies for satisfying those yearnings (our sin in *demanding* that people be there for us).

It is essential to face both our pain and our sin; one without the other will result in imbalance and injury to the marriage. If we're willing to look at our pain of having been let down by others but are unwilling to look at our sinful strategies for protecting ourselves without relying on God, then our truth-telling will likely result in either bitterness or a pursuit of some method for relieving our pain.

We have been not only victims of others' inability to love us perfectly but also agents who have moved aggressively to protect ourselves from their unlove in any way we can. Looking at the pain of past and present disappointments must move us to see the pattern of our sin in dealing with those disappointments. As Dr. Larry Crabb points out,

> Certainly we struggle as victims of other people's unkindness. We have been sinned against. But we cannot excuse our sinful responses to others on grounds of their mistreatment of us. We are responsible for what we do. We are both strugglers and sinners, victims and agents, people who hurt and people who harm.[2]

If we are honest about our sin but refuse to open ourselves to the pain of past and present realities, the result will be surface living. Our behavior may change (we may try harder to stop sinning externally with our mates), but our inner selves will remain untouched and the relationship will be shallow at best. Meaningful change requires tears of hurt and tears of repentance as we risk honesty with ourselves, with God, and with our spouses.

Honesty with Ourselves
Self-honesty requires that we speak the truth to ourselves about the hard-to-face realities of our lives. We must face the pain caused by the sins of others, beginning with an honest look at our past.

Some people must acknowledge their legitimate disappointment at the absence of childhood intimacy with their parents. Adult victims of childhood incest or abuse or alcoholic family dysfunction, for example, have usually built barriers around their memories to block out certain childhood traumas. Although their memories were blocked, their emotions didn't go away, and unattended past disappointments (because they taught wrong ways to handle present relationships) must be faced, perhaps with the help of a Christian counselor.

Not everyone, thankfully, must struggle with having been abused as a child. But all of us were born to imperfect parents, and no one is immune from hurtful events that occurred during the growing-up years. Even those of us schooled in silence about our pain as children must learn to tell ourselves the truth about past woundedness.

We must face our disappointments not to justify our anger or to take revenge against those who hurt us in the past. Rather, we must face the pain to discover what we did as children to *avoid* the pain and protect ourselves from further suffering. Our mechanisms for avoiding disappointment in our early relationships often become the self-protective patterns we use throughout our lives to keep ourselves safe in later relationships. Thus, facing our childhood pain is useful for driving us to the Father and also for exposing our self-protective strategies in current relationships.

We must also face the pain of present circumstances, especially in our marriages. Because we were designed to be perfectly loved (a design twisted by the Fall), we experience disappointment with our mates, though to differing degrees. Sometimes, "intimacy" is purchased at the expense of honesty in a Christian marriage, both spouses ignoring real problems and genuine pain with the vague hope that somehow their "spirituality" will both cover and heal what is amiss in the relationship. Facing marital disappointment takes determination. It was an awful crisis for my husband and me. A lot was at stake, and we were haunted with some unsettling questions: Did I marry the right person? What if our marriage doesn't survive? What if it does? How is our son, Chris, going to manage this trauma?

When partners move toward increasing health in their marriage, they must begin by looking honestly at circumstances as they are, not as they wish they were or think they should be. They must be honest about their present as well as their past pain in intimate relationships because the strategies they developed as children for keeping themselves safe are usually repeating themselves in the marriage. Facing present pain helps them see what they are doing now to self-protect instead of love.

It's not enough, though, to be honest about our suffering. We must also speak truthfully to ourselves about our sin, the deep inner bentness of our attempts to keep ourselves out of pain. We'd like to justify our anger against those who have let us down. Often anger (especially the normal anger at having been abused or neglected) is a necessary part of our healing process. But anger should not be our destination; it should represent stops along the way to healing. Throughout the journey, even in our anger, we must look honestly at the self-protective ways we continually avoid our pain by using others (particularly our spouses) to make ourselves feel good instead of loving them as God commanded. With the help of the Holy Spirit we must face our failure to love as the sin God named it to be.

Honesty with God

Thus, honesty with ourselves in our marriages must be accompanied by honesty with God, entering His presence and opening our true selves to Him. My parents taught me to pray as a child, yet even into adulthood I mostly spoke to God in whitewashed words. However, when I began feeling the pain of my past and present disappointments, I started really *talking* to God, not just mouthing pleasant prayers. I cried and complained and shouted. I was not nice, but I was me—the real me, not the antiseptic me I'd always thought I had to be in His presence.

And, wonderfully, I was heard and loved. Like the psalmists of old, I learned to cry out my true feelings, and I discovered that God could bear the weight of my soul. Scripture records honestly the sometimes shocking inner realities of men like David and Jonah and Job. If even Jesus could cry out, "My God, my God, why have you forsaken me?" (Matthew 27:46), then surely we can voice the agony of our pain to the Father.

But we must also learn to stand unclothed in God's presence and deal honestly with our sin as the Holy Spirit gives us eyes to see things clearly. How we hate to do that, fearing the shame of His disappointed look at our deep failure to be the lovers He has called us to be! Yet how profoundly we need to be undressed of our filthy rags of presumed righteousness in order to find ourselves reclothed with Christ, to know we are seen with eyes of love, naked but unashamed in the purifying burning of His perfect love and holiness.

If we will not risk the rejection we fear from Holy God, we will not know our fear cast out by His forgiving love when we repent. We must speak to God the truth (how ludicrous to think He could not already know) of our pain and of our honest agreement with Him about our self-protective unlove so we can repent, experience His grace, and learn to love each other in the right way.

Honesty with Our Partners

Honesty with ourselves and with God can be excruciating, but honesty with our partners is usually the hardest. The possibility of rejection in our most intimate relationship somehow feels more frightening than exposure to the eyes of a holy but loving God. Even as we grow in our knowledge that our security and adequacy rest in the Father, we nonetheless look for (even depend on) reassurances from each other.

Though I've been doing my truth-telling calisthenics for several years now, I still have anxiety attacks when I must tell Bill honestly what's going on inside me. In fact, the better our relationship is at the time, the more I fear his anger or disapproval (who wants to lose the warm fuzzies?) and the more exacting it is to speak the truth. Truth-telling with our mates is no small risk; their possible rejection at the base of our safe cliff can easily frighten us into not jumping.

KNOWING WHAT TO BE HONEST ABOUT

Once we gather the courage to speak the truth, we struggle to know what to be honest about. It isn't hard to say what we like about each other, though we often neglect to do so. Appropriate truth-telling about our disappointments in the relationship is more difficult. Usually when we are in pain because of our spouses' sin, we either attack or retreat, and each response blocks true intimacy.

So what should we do? Should we tell them the truth about how awful we think they are? Should we express our disgust or hatred toward them? How do we balance ourselves on the delicate tightrope between integrity about our feelings and sensitivity to theirs?

GIVING I-MESSAGES

In confronting the pain of a spouse's unlove, an individual ought to give what Dr. Thomas Gordon in his book *Teacher Effectiveness Training* calls "I-messages."[3] I-messages are sentences about how *I* am feeling or reacting to an event or communication in contrast to you-messages, which communicate an evaluation of *you* for your actions.

An I-message communicates the effect of my spouse's actions or words on me (taking responsibility for honesty about my feelings) rather than how I think my spouse ought to change to please me (taking responsibility for his behavior). The focus of I-messages is not on my spouse's sin ("You sure didn't act like much of a Christian tonight") but on how that sin has affected me ("I needed you to be there for me, and I was hurt when you weren't"). I must say what is true about my inner life, without using "honesty" to either demolish my spouse's self-esteem or take responsibility for changing him.

I-messages are scary because they open our true selves to the scrutiny, and possible rejection, of our mates. It is risky business to gradually drop our emotional anonymity and expose ourselves to our spouses. They may think us silly or may even be glad at their success in having hurt us. Yet God has called us to shed our cloaks of pride and fear and reveal (and thus thwart) established strategies of self-protection so we can become better lovers.

When one believer offends another, they must deal with the offense in order to be reconciled. Jesus advised, "If your brother sins against you, go and show him his fault. . . . If he listens to you, you have won your brother over" (Matthew 18:15). And the writer of Hebrews warned against letting undealt-with anger escalate into bitterness: "See to it that . . . no bitter root grows up to cause trouble and defile many" (Hebrews 12:15). Telling our spouses about our pain over their sin reflects obedience to God's plan for His people, and we must persevere in removing our masks even though our mates may refuse to receive those messages or respond with godly sorrow so that reconciliation can occur.

I-messages are difficult to speak. But surprisingly, I-messages actually offer a higher probability of being received than you-messages. Both wives and husbands long for true intimacy, and I-messages remove the sting of the judgmentalism and criticism of you-messages, which often block intimacy. In a fallen world, it would be dishonest to speak only complimentary things to or about our mates. Ignoring or condoning their sin is not God's way of loving them, nor should it be ours. It is the *impact on us* of our mates' sin that we must speak, not our condemnation of them as sinners. That is a significant distinction.

DECIDING WHETHER TO TELL THE TRUTH

A further problem involves the issue of when to speak and when not to speak. This is not merely a matter of timing, though we probably need a periodic reminder that just before dinner is rarely a good time to talk about matters of consequence. Rather, it is a question of whether to speak at all, which can often be determined by how much we fear the consequences of our truth-telling. A spouse's anxiety about giving an I-message is a clue that silence may be the self-protective strategy keeping him or her from loving, in which case the truth probably *should* be told. Asking why we are not speaking the truth will help us to decide whether to speak up or not.

I recently overheard a woman at a party interrupt her husband's joke to announce that each of his stories took so long to tell, it would delay the coming of Christmas. Her comment got a laugh, but he didn't seem to find it funny. I wonder what he said during their drive home. Knowing her, I suspect he probably kept his silence to remain safe from her tongue. That is exactly why he should have dropped his self-protection by risking an I-message like, "I felt angry about your comment tonight. I feel so demeaned when you belittle me in front of our friends." His response would undoubtedly have heightened the tension between them and might not have resulted in her becoming less critical, but at least he would have offered to her his real self, which would have been more loving than his self-protection.

Condoning or indulging sin in our mates by our silence shows them no love. Ignoring their wrongdoing usually indicates fear for our personal safety (not concern for them) and a deep disrespect of their ability to handle honest confrontation. For example, when a woman tells her husband that his workaholism leaves her and their children without the strong emotional support they need, she shows him deep respect. Telling the truth about sin and its impact on us is a strong movement toward loving our mates the way God loves us.

Learning to give I-messages is a long-term process that does not happen comfortably if it has not been happening all along in a relationship. I found it very demanding to speak and hear the truth about the underlying realities of my relationship with Bill. He didn't like the truth I offered him about myself, nor did I like what he told me. Both of us would have preferred our familiar pretenses.

But spouses who increasingly understand their own and their mates' legitimate needs for genuine respect and ungrudging love will embrace the risk of truth-telling, even when the truth is hard to speak and hard to receive. Continuing honesty about our perceptions and feelings, even when our I-messages fall on deaf ears or elicit an angry response, is a mark of genuine repentance for the self-protective lies that often characterize our relationships.

CONFESSING SIN

Another important element in telling the truth to our marriage partners is our handling of the sin in our lives. We must learn not only to confront but also to confess. James urges believers, "Confess your sins to each other" (James 5:16). Certainly as spouses, we should follow his advice.

I discovered early in my revival process that I had a lot of repenting to do for some big-time control strategies I had been employing for years. As I progressed in my confessing, I became more and more sensitive to my "little" sins as well—like shading the truth to avoid a confrontation.

On one occasion after telling Bill I was meeting a friend for supper because it was the only evening we could get together, I had to turn the car around and go back to tell him the *real* reason I was meeting her. I was in so much pain in our marriage then that I felt I would die if I didn't talk to someone about it. Mine had been only a little lie, but I needed to root it out because it was part of my pattern for staying safe and avoiding being real with Bill. One step at a time I had to confess my real pain and my real sin to him.

It's unfortunate that one spouse often refuses to confess unless the other spouse confesses first. Not wanting to let a mate off the hook, an individual won't acknowledge even a percentage of responsibility for what went wrong. Unfortunately, the mate who first risks honest confession usually *does* receive more blame initially, so that acknowledging true guilt (i.e., becoming nondefensive about sin) feels like abdicating.

Yet even when the other one does not repent and change, the growing spouse must continue confessing, taking comfort in the knowledge that his or her repentance has opened the way to grace and has restored fellowship with the Father, if not with the partner. Moreover, the confessing spouse must resist the temptation to ease the tension by taking more responsibility than is deserved. God holds us accountable for acknowledging only our guilt, not someone else's.

DISTINGUISHING NEEDS FROM WANTS

One final aspect of truth-telling concerns defining the goal of honesty. Paul instructed the Ephesian Christians to speak "the truth *in love*" (Ephesians 4:15, emphasis added). If our honesty is not moving us toward learning to better love each other, it is not what Paul had in mind. In marriage, truth-telling with *agape* love means that we minister not to whatever our spouses *want*, but according to what our spouses *need*.

Needs and wants are not synonymous. Our teenage son may *want* a motorcycle, but he *needs* a sturdy used car. God knows we *want* to run our lives our own way, but He also knows we *need* to be saved unto holy living for His glory. Many wives *want* to stay in control in their marriages, but they *need* to become responders in the relationship. Many husbands *want* to either dominate or retreat from their wives, but they *need* to act like the strong and loving men God calls them to be. When wives respect their husbands and husbands involve themselves with their wives by confronting in love the sinful control and retreat patterns they see, the goal must be to draw each other toward repentance and forgiveness so that the relationship can be brought back into balance. He is to lead, and she is to submit to his leadership.

The Christian community has for too long misinterpreted love as being a namby-pamby niceness that never makes waves or steps on anyone's toes. According to that way of thinking, Christians should never speak any truth that would offend or upset someone else. How unlike Jesus' expressions of love! Being God, He always spoke the truth in love, yet His truth-telling often offended others, including those He loved most. He always ministered to what people needed (the truth about their sin that would draw them to repentance and forgiveness), not to what they wanted (to hear nice words about how wonderful they were). People's expectations were never the determining factor in what He said or did. He always confronted sin in a way that His hearers could receive it (though not all did). And when they refused to hear Him, He grieved (Matthew 23:37) but went on loving them anyway, all the way to the cross.

We, too, must love the way Jesus loved, according to people's needs, not their wants. And like Him, we may experience people's rejection of us and of the truth we tell. What if we become honest and our spouses just don't care about the impact their sin has on us? Why go through the pain if nothing ever changes or the situation only gets worse? Then we must do as Jesus did when He looked out over Jerusalem, whose inhabitants would reject Him unto death. He didn't run from the pain. He felt it and wept, not just for His loss but for what they would lose because of their unbelief (Luke 19:41-44).

When our spouses refuse our offer of honesty and strong love, we can turn to Jesus in our pain, knowing that "we do not have a high priest who is unable to sympathize with our weaknesses, but we have one who has been tempted in every way, just as we are—yet was without sin" (Hebrews 4:15). Perhaps we, like Jesus, will have to face the searing pain of our beloved's rejection of our honest loving—maybe even the pain of losing the relationship altogether. But we, like Jesus, can choose to love in spite of the pain and pour out our lives for our marriage partners in the Spirit's strength even when we're not experiencing any love in return. Jesus promised we would find real *life* if we abandon ourselves to Him (Matthew 16:25). He will ultimately bring us to see that being alive in Him is worth enduring any cross because of the joy that awaits us at Home (Hebrews 12:1-3).

SUMMING UP

Loving our spouses, then, means that we will tell the truth about our pain and our sin to ourselves, to God, and to our partners. Sometimes the truth can be seen and expressed on all three levels almost simultaneously. For example, if Bill made an unkind remark to me, I might let myself feel the pain of his words, acknowledge internally my wrong desire to retreat emotionally from him, and repent before God of my sinful self-protection. Then I might risk telling Bill how injured I'd felt by his remark and ask him to forgive me for retreating from him. That would involve honesty (about both my pain and my sin) with myself, with God, and with him.

More often, however, especially in the early steps of our change process, the truth can be seen, acknowledged, and expressed only in small increments and over a much longer period of time. Like the muscles in our bodies that are developed through physical exercise, our honesty muscles must be built up gradually and with considerable effort and discomfort. Truth-telling at all three levels usually does not happen all at once. Sometimes we can face our pain but not our sin. Or we might admit our sin to ourselves and God but not have the courage to be honest with our mates. The goal is that over time we develop our honesty muscles in all three areas so that we more often exhibit a lifestyle of honest interaction in our marriages, living out what the *NIV Study Bible* calls "a truthful and loving manner of life."[4]

NOTES:
1. R.C. Sproul, *The Intimate Marriage* (Wheaton, Ill.: Tyndale House Publishers, 1986), page 9.
2. Larry Crabb, *Inside Out* (Colorado Springs, Colo.: NavPress, 1988), page 132.
3. Thomas Gordon, *Teacher Effectiveness Training* (New York: Peter H. Wyden, Publisher, 1974), pages 136-155.
4. *The NIV Study Bible*, Kenneth Barker ed. (Grand Rapids: Zondervan Bible Publishers, 1985), page 1796.

QUESTIONS FOR THOUGHT AND DISCUSSION

1. Tell yourself the truth about one painful memory from your childhood.

2. How would you like to have been comforted in that circumstance?

3. What did you do to protect yourself in that circumstance?

4. Be honest with yourself about one painful thing in your marriage. Explain how you feel about it.

5. In what ways are you sinfully protecting yourself in that circumstance?

6. If you tell the truth about how your mate's sin affects you, what "I-message" can you give him (or her)?

7. Allow the Holy Spirit to convict you of your present failure to love your mate in the right way. What words of confession can you speak to him (or her)?

11

CLAW REMOVAL:
Letting Go

The woman speaking to the support group for families of substance abusers was strikingly attractive, silver hair beautifully in place, elegant fingers brightly manicured, serenity shining from behind lovely blue eyes. She was describing her experience of having four children addicted to drugs and of feeling totally helpless to change her circumstances. She went on to say that hers was a recovery story—her own recovery, that is. She discovered that the only life for which she could take responsibility was her own, and over time she learned to release her obsessive control over her children's lives. Forming her slender hands into witch's talons, she drew them back toward her shoulders, saying, "I had to remove my claws, let my children make their own choices, then let them live with the consequences of those choices."

My friend's curled fingers graphically portrayed my desperate attempts to control the people in my life, especially Bill. Skewered on my claws, he had little choice but to yield to my "advice" and pressure. Yet no matter how sweetly I managed his life, he resented me for it, and I don't blame him. I reacted similarly to his self-protective withdrawal from me through his silence or quiet anger. We both tried to stay safe from and to manipulate each other through our control and retreat mechanisms, and we needed to repent by letting go of those strategies. They were potentially fatal to our marriage.

Injecting new health into marriage requires two calisthenics: telling the truth in love and learning to let go of "managing" our spouses. Our psychological muscles of mutual self-protection often atrophy in the talons-in position, and it is no easy chore withdrawing our claws and releasing our "prey." Old habits die hard, especially in trying to change long-cherished self-protective strategies.

RECOGNIZING OUR STYLE

What does self-protection look like in a marriage? At the risk of oversimplification, let's name the two main styles as the husband's retreat and the wife's control. A man's primary self-protective strategy (in violation of his responsibility to move strongly toward his wife with loving leadership) is to give in to his fear of inadequacy by backing away from decisive action or intimate involvement or both. Not sure of his competence, he settles for minimizing his opportunities to fail by staying away.

This male retreat can masquerade as cruel demandingness (a retreat from sacrificial loving), passive indecision (a retreat from strong leadership), or a behavioral style somewhere in between. However a husband's retreat evidences itself, it is rooted in a fear of relational inadequacy and is directed toward protection from his wife's refusal to respond to his leadership with submission and respect.

On the other hand, a woman's primary self-protection (in violation of her call to respond to her husband) is to yield to her fear of exploitation and rejection by trying to control her world. Unsure that she is lovable, she settles for minimizing her opportunities to be hurt by staying in charge. A wife's control might look like helpless dependence (a barometer woman being irresponsible, demanding that her husband take care of her), drill-sergeant efficiency (an appeasing or manipulative woman running her own life her way), or a behavioral style somewhere in between. No matter how subtle or blatant, a wife's control is rooted in fear of abandonment and is directed toward self-protection from her husband's failure to love.

When a wife controls (the perversion of a husband's leadership) and her husband retreats (the perversion of a wife's responsiveness), they are failing to love each other as they should and they must repent. If they would deeply heal their marriage, they must manifest their repentance by removing the claws of control and abandoning the retreat strategies that have kept them "protected" and distant from God and from each other.

TAKING RESPONSIBILITY FOR PERSONAL CHANGE

As we practice letting go of our self-protection, we must distinguish between what we can and cannot control. We are accountable for changes in *our* thinking and behavior, but we must not take responsibility for the changes we hope our mates will make, though we may desire and fervently pray for them. Every spouse has tried to orchestrate changes in his or her partner (always in the other's best interest, of course). Engaged couples always believe that after the wedding their influence will accomplish personality and character renovations in each other. Unfortunately, it seldom works, and if it does, the person's freedom is violated.

The primary reason for distinguishing between what we can and cannot control is that most spouses focus their energy on trying to change the self-protective strategies of their mates. In a vicious cycle of mutual manipulation, a husband resists his wife's attempts to control him, and she tries to prevent his retreat or force his involvement with her. Each tries to change the other's wrong strategies instead of dropping his or her own. Removing the claws of control and abandoning retreat means that we turn the spotlight of both our heart changes and our behavioral changes away from our mates and back on ourselves.

SEEING OURSELVES A NEW WAY

How is it possible for us to genuinely drop our masks and live without our comfortable control and retreat mechanisms? If we are to live free and love appropriately, we must learn to see ourselves in a new way, the way the Father sees us. Paul teaches that "if anyone is in Christ, he is a new creation; the old has gone, the new has come!" (2 Corinthians 5:17). The implications of being a "new creation" are far-reaching, but one aspect is that, in Christ, God sees us as already perfect. We are the initiating husbands and responsive wives He designed men and women to be in the first place. Moreover, through the sanctifying power of His indwelling Holy Spirit, He enables us to increasingly resemble in our everyday actions who we already are in His eyes.

The model for our redeemed humanity is Jesus, who perfectly patterned both initiating maleness (toward His Bride, the Church) and responsive femaleness (in His submission to the Father) during His life on earth. Both His initiating love and His responsive submission flowed from the reality that He was infinitely beloved of the Father and lived in such intimate fellowship with Him that He could sacrificially pour out His life to meet His people's needs by gladly conforming to His Father's will.

John wrote that Jesus washed His disciples' feet because He "knew that the Father had put all things under his power, and that he had come from God and was returning to God" (John 13:3). Jesus did not need to prove His worth. From a position of legitimate strength, He chose to use His power for service. He knew who He was and to whom He belonged and what the Father had called and empowered Him to do. And knowing that—in fact, *because* of that—He readied Himself to clean the dirty feet of those He loved. Jesus is the model for redeemed husbands of every age.

Paul expressed the same idea when he noted that Jesus humbled Himself unto death in the context of knowing He was "in very nature God" yet "did not consider equality with God something to be grasped" (Philippians 2:6). Christ's servanthood flowed from His recognition of His true nature and value. His strength was brought under submission to His Father for the purpose of serving the elect. Redeemed wives can exercise submission from a similar position of strength.

How different Jesus' posture is from the reasons and ways we usually relate to each other in our marriages! So often husbands demonstrate not Christlike strength, being willing to sacrifice, but fearful inadequacy either bullying its way or refusing to risk. And so many wives manifest not Christ's dignity, offering their strength to bless, but a spirit of either self-contempt ("Mistreat me, I deserve it") or imperiousness ("Do things my way, or you'll pay").

We don't have to stay bound to our retreat and control manipulations. Because we are in Christ, we can know ourselves beloved of the

Father, and in that self-knowledge, we can increasingly relinquish our strategies and choose to minister to our spouses' needs by behaving as the adequate husbands and responsive wives we already are. God calls us to "put on" our redeemed male or female nature as we drop self-protection in our marriages. We no longer have anything to prove. We can stop clawing after our rights, because we know who we are and to whom we belong and why we are here in the first place—to pour out our lives for each other, not from deficit but from the overflow of Christ's life in us.

ABANDONING CONTROL AND RETREAT

What changes should we make as the strong men and esteemed women we are in Christ, living out repentance of our self-protective strategies? What should we do differently to move us away from our obsession with our own happiness and instead minister to the need of the one to whom we are covenantally bound? How do we remove our claws of control and abandon our strategies of retreat?

The danger of the how-to section of any book is that no two people are alike. One person's self-protective strategy never exactly duplicates anyone else's because everyone has unique parents, a unique childhood, and unique adolescent and adult experiences. Furthermore, two differing self-protective strategies come together in a marriage, so no two marriages are ever alike, either. Thus, no how-to advice can be universally applicable except in broad generalizations. What specifically must change will depend on what specifically is wrong. Each spouse must read the following suggestions and recognize his or her particular strategies of self-protection. Claw removal, like truth-telling, is an individual sport.

A WIFE'S REPENTANCE OF HER CONTROL

In the first section of this book, we isolated three patterns of feminine control masquerading as submission: absorption, appeasement, and manipulation. Though certainly not an exhaustive list, these patterns model some of the more common ways wives try to take charge in their marriages so they can stay out of pain. What behaviors will each type of wife adopt as she genuinely repents of her self-protective control?

The Barometer Wife

A barometer wife who controls her circumstances by becoming absorbed in her husband will begin to repent of her self-protective helplessness when she stops believing her negative sentences about herself and faces the truth of her value in Christ. Dropping her defensive strategies of self-contempt will be uncomfortable, but she must repent of belittling herself and work toward offering herself as a woman of substance to her husband. What kinds of behaviors will flow out of a barometer wife's repentance?

Perhaps she will have to practice asking for and receiving what she needs from her husband as an expression of her legitimate value. Or she will accept her God-given responsibility for becoming the best she can be by choosing to develop a talent or improve her appearance or go back to school—whatever will enhance her inner strengths and increase her experience of her worth and usefulness to Christ's Kingdom.

Also, as soon and as often as she dares, she should probably disagree verbally with her husband—kindly, if possible—whenever there is an honest difference of opinion. It will not be easy, but the barometer wife must face her terrifying conviction that if her husband rejected or left her, she would cease to exist. To genuinely repent, she will have to more frequently offer him the real person within and risk his disapproval to show him genuine respect.

The Appeasing Wife

The repentance of an appeasing wife will look altogether different than that of a barometer wife. Her control through appeasement must gradually give way to realizing that because God is the sovereign Protector of her inner life, she can stop trying to orchestrate everything in her marriage. She must change her goal from keeping her husband happy, whatever the cost, to doing what is good for him (which may make him more unhappy for a while). What things will an appeaser do to live out her repentance?

For one thing, she'll probably stop trying to prevent her husband from doing wrong or looking bad and let him make his own choices and then handle the consequences. Once I caught myself literally trying to shush Bill because he was talking more angrily than I thought he should in a social situation. (How *motherly* of me!) I had to tell him later, "I will no longer be custodian of your anger. You can handle it however you want, and I won't interfere." He was delighted, and I was relieved. Though he didn't immediately become less angry, eventually I came to enjoy not having knots in my stomach when we were with other people.

An appeasing wife will ask the Holy Spirit to help her discern her legitimate responsibility in the family, and then she will forgo what is not her job. Over time she will know which marital hills are worth dying on; that is, she will identify which things she absolutely will not take responsibility for, even if they remain undone. She will probably also encourage her husband to interact with the children instead of protecting them from one another—unless the children are in danger. And she will likely risk her husband's anger by expressing her true feelings when his behavior is unbiblical, especially if it is abusive or addictive. If he resists her change process (and he will), she will give up managing even his resistance.

This repentance to noncontrol will feel like death to an appeaser. When Bill and I began our roller-coaster ride of change and reaction, our world was turned topsy-turvy. I was terrorized by my absolute dependence on Christ to carry me through each day. Previously, I'd always depended on *me*. But ministering to Bill's need for respect and submission (not his desire for a hassle-free existence) meant that I had to turn to God and then sever each string by which I had kept Bill a marionette dancing to my tune. An appeaser's repentance will seem like capitulation from responsibility, but it will really be a godly willingness to trust the Father with her inner life while she lets go of her emasculating control and learns she doesn't need peace in her external circumstances to survive.

The Manipulating Wife

A manipulating wife is often more blatant in her marital control, but as is true of her barometer and appeasing sisters, her self-protection is rooted in fear. What new behaviors will demonstrate a manipulator's repentance?

In giving up her attempts to remake her husband, she'll probably stop feeding him clues about how to behave or writing the script of his life. Instead she'll learn to wait for him to act or speak on his own. If she has always checked up on him, she'll stop that, too, and ask God to show her what she needs to know and when. If she has been the decision-maker, she will ask her husband to decide, and she'll be willing to accept his decisions. If he absolutely refuses to take that responsibility, she will have to seek the Spirit's help to know in which areas she absolutely must intervene in order to keep the family functioning.

Perhaps a manipulating wife will express her repentance by facing and verbalizing her legitimate need for her husband's involvement. She won't have to pretend to be weak, but she will risk his rejection by letting herself feel her legitimate longing for his love and protection. Neediness is repulsive to controlling women, who usually feel shamed by their need and commit themselves to emotional independence from others, especially their husbands. Yet a woman is right to yearn for intimacy with her chosen mate, though she ought not demand that he provide it.

Paradoxically, when a manipulating woman realizes she needs her husband, she opens herself to the pain of his retreat (her greatest fear), and she will feel driven to make him say or do what she now thinks she cannot live without. I have known what it's like to face Bill's rejection in the context of my acknowledged need for him. It wasn't easy to need and also live without Bill's tender involvement as part of God's plan for me. But I learned in the process to surrender myself more and more during that time to the Father who was always there for me with His perfect strength and dependable love.

One other reality a manipulating wife may have to face is her husband's becoming the strong man she thought she wanted him to be. I recently wrote in my journal: "A free Bill is a frightening Bill, though the woman in me deeply needs and desires it. I ought to be glad about his freedom from my manipulation but I'm not; I feel angry and afraid. I fear my loss of control over him."

Power pleases, and giving up my emotional power over Bill was a loss for which I grieved as for a familiar friend. It had to die, this control of mine, but I hated to see it go. My consolation was the Father's pleasure at my letting go and the taste I got of how good it would be to live with a man I couldn't manage.

A repenting manipulator's real work begins when her husband repents of his retreat and begins to move into her life with confident strength. That is when she will know whether or not she really wants to become the responder God has called her to be.

A HUSBAND'S REPENTANCE FOR HIS RETREAT

Wives must repent of their self-protective control mechanisms in their marriages, but their husbands hide, too—usually behind some retreat strategies. What must a husband do to repent of his self-protective withdrawal, rooted in his fear of inadequacy? Again, it depends on the nature of his individual sin pattern. Even the two broad categories we will cover (tryannical retreat and passive retreat) have an infinite variety of behavioral manifestations, and each man must acknowledge his peculiar pattern of self-protection in order to know how to change. His repentance, however, must reflect Jesus' servanthood, and his new behaviors must flow from his recognition of his value and adequacy as a redeemed man made in God's image. A repentant husband can act more like the strong, loving man he already is in Christ.

The Tyrannical Husband

The husband who is cruel to his wife, physically or verbally, operates not from godly concern for his wife's welfare but from fear of her criticism. His tyranny indicates insecurity not strength. Often his wife instinctively knows this, yet she accommodates his insecure abuse out of emasculating pity toward him. Such a man must recognize that his cruelty protects him from his wife. Then in the strength of knowing he is already a loved, adequate man in Christ, he can repent and begin to change his destructive patterns. What will his repentance look like?

Surely he will stop his abusive behavior and seek help from a counselor and/or support group if necessary. Perhaps he will also initiate kindness and gentle involvement with his wife, looking for ways to encourage and build her up. Instead of having to prove her wrong (in order to prove himself right), he will practice confessing his own wrongdoing to her. If she asks him for something, he probably should try to give it to her, though he will feel weak when he does so— and looking weak is what he most dreads. As his strength becomes increasingly grounded in the Spirit's sanctifying work, he will become less invested in bossing his wife and more adept at esteeming her.

Whether or not his wife appreciates the change in him or responds to him right away (or ever), a repentant tyrannical husband will be able to love her anyway. She may need time to work through her (appropriate) anger at past abuse, but over time the Spirit's presence will enable him to persevere in his loving involvement with her, in spite of the disappointment he may feel.

The Passive Husband

A passive and indecisive husband, on the other hand, will practice different things in living out his repentance. Like the cruel husband, his self-protection is rooted in his fear of failing at leadership, but his marital style is to let his wife have her own way. Sometimes he even *insists* that she take the lead. Bill and I have talked about how frightening it is for him to break free of my manipulative strategies. He feels safer not risking being strong for me, even though that is really what he wants (and what I want).

When a passive husband repents, he will begin by believing more certainly that his manhood is secure in Christ so he can start acting with greater confidence (through risk) like the strong leader he already is. What behaviors will characterize the repentant lifestyle of a passive husband?

Probably he will risk being more assertive about things and even willing to fail because he knows his inner life with Christ will not be destroyed. He'll deliberately stop hiding behind whatever has been keeping him safe, such as silence, the newspaper, humor, Scripture-quoting, or blame-shifting. Looking past his insecurity, a repentant passive husband will discern what his wife needs in the way of strong leadership and give that to her without making her pay for it later (by reminding her, for example, of how much it cost him to do it). He'll ask for fewer clues from his wife and initiate involvement with her without being asked. (I loved it when Bill planned a surprise overnight celebration of our anniversary at one of the classiest hotels in town.)

Or a repentant "pacifist" will repent by accepting his share of the blame when things go wrong and apologizing for what is his fault. Instead of running from his mistake, he will dare to admit and ask forgiveness for his failure to love, knowing he is already forgiven by the Father because of Jesus' sacrifice.

A passive man will undoubtedly have to risk failure in lots of small and large ways, and it will feel like death to him. But because he will have to depend on God for his adequacy in the midst of every risk he takes, that "death" will be his way to life. Though his wife may resist or ultimately refuse to gladly submit to his leadership, in the process of his change, her unsubmissiveness will gradually lose its power to destroy him because his inner life will be hidden with Christ in God. He will know pain in the process, but he will emerge a strong and godly man in spite of the pain—perhaps even because of it.

SUMMING UP

A husband and wife who will dare to risk abandoning retreat and removing the claws of control must begin by discerning their unique masks behind which they have hidden to keep themselves somewhat safe and their marriage relationship mostly sterile. Then they must genuinely repent of their self-protective motives and behavior, and they must take responsibility for changing themselves, not each other.

As they look to Jesus' example of servanthood, they must increasingly recognize and live out their value and worth in God's eyes as redeemed image-bearers who can and who desire to do the Father's will. Then their heart-motivated behavioral changes must fly in the face of their greatest fears, custom-designed repentance for their customized self-protection. They must make these changes with increasing consistency and perseverance, ungrudgingly and from the heart. They must do these things even though they know ahead of time that when they are being the most repentant in their actions toward each other, they will feel the most terrified and appalled.

Such repentance will not happen unless spouses are willing to live in wholehearted dependence on God and to commit to probably several years of making these changes—with all of life's usual ups and downs, successes and failures, trials and errors, good days and bad.

The boat will most certainly be rocked for a while, and some marriages may never recover or achieve their balance. But the process of abandoning the mechanisms of retreat and removing the claws of control will force spouses to stretch their spiritual muscles as never before and grow in an intimacy with and reflection of Christ that is, after all, His ultimate intention for everyone.

QUESTIONS FOR THOUGHT AND DISCUSSION

1. Think of a marriage you know well and explain how the wife may be controlling and the husband retreating.

2. Describe what you'd like to change in your partner that God may be calling you to relinquish as an act of repentance.

3. If you are a wife, identify which category best describes your marriage style (barometer, appeasing, or manipulating). What behaviors illustrate that style?

4. What specifically can you do as a wife to remove your claws of control (according to the style you described in the previous question) and give love to your husband?

5. If you are a husband, which category—tyrannical or passive—best describes your primary marriage style? Name your behaviors that evidence that style.

6. Indicate the specific actions you, as a husband, can take to abandon your pattern of retreat (according to the style you described in the previous question) and give love to your wife.

4

FREEDOM:
Discarding the Masks

12

INNER DYNAMICS:
The Spirit of a Marriage

Christians often evaluate the health of a marriage by its degree of conformity to role expectations of submission and headship, and these expectations are often bound to who-does-what-in-the-marriage kinds of questions. Such questions, however, frequently miss the real issues in actual marriage situations.

Most submission-authority conflicts in a marriage have little or nothing to do with determining, for example, who will break the tie in a marital impasse. Wives and husbands struggle with appropriate submission and authority in a much deeper way, which is related to who they are as men and women. Where to go for dinner and who should balance the checkbook and whether or not to move to another state are really minor issues in the grand scheme of things. A husband's initiating authority and his wife's responsive submission are revealed not in the roles they play or are expected to play, but in the inner dynamics of what passes between their spirits.

A wife's submission and a husband's authority are ultimately choices that will emerge unerringly from each one's spirit. The heart attitude determines the quality of the relationship. Proverbs 4:23 warns, "Above all else, guard your heart, for it is the wellspring of life."

Jesus' comment applies particularly in a marriage: "The good man brings good things out of the good stored up in his heart, and the evil man brings evil things out of the evil stored up in his heart. For out of the overflow of his heart his mouth speaks" (Luke 6:45). Thus, each partner gives to the other what is in the heart.

The heart cannot remain secret. The public image of a marriage can be convincingly congenial, and even on the family level, it can look pretty good. But in the deep inner workings of the marriage, each spouse instinctively knows whether the other's heart is devoted or divided. Sometimes longstanding pretense or a desperate need to maintain an illusion of intimacy may make one or both partners deny the sundering they sense in their spirits. But in some way they know what is true, because out of the overflow of what is really in the heart they communicate with each other. Truth, as they say, will always come out.

A WIFE'S WRONG SPIRIT

A woman's behavior may belie her true spirit, but her husband almost always knows and responds to what is really going on. Often her dissatisfaction with how things are in the marriage—compared to how they might be or could have been—comes out in subtle ways her husband cannot miss.

Hostile Dependence
Many barometer wives, however meek their external behavior, foster a spirit of hostile dependence. This spirit is the equivalent of a wife saying to her husband, "I am dependent on you, but I despise it and hate you for it." Such women often believe themselves unable to make it financially or emotionally without being married, and their spirits communicate an unwilling, forced subjugation, not glad submission. A man is stripped of his manhood when his wife holds in contempt her dependence on him, and her camouflaged hostility cannot be hidden from his spirit.

Pseudo-dependence
An appeasing wife, on the other hand, may appear appropriately dependent on her husband, but her managing spirit carries this

message: "You are incompetent to handle this, so I'll just take care of it for you." Moreover, as she closes herself off emotionally and refuses to show she is wounded by his hurtful words or actions (except by playing the martyr), she communicates to him: "You are too unimportant to affect me at all. I can live equally well with or without your kindness because you are not worth taking into account." Her husband receives her unspoken disrespect in his spirit and is influenced by it.

For years I pretended indifference to Bill's unkindnesses. But when I began to respond appropriately by bleeding emotionally (i.e., verbalizing my pain) any time he cut me with his words, my new message to him was, "What you say reaches who I am because you matter—enough to either hurt me or please me." Though he often responded defensively—he preferred the "old Nancy" who didn't rock the boat or hold him accountable for his comments—I was at least no longer being false about my genuine need for his cherishing and protection.

Antidependence

Sometimes what a man picks up in the spirit of his manipulating wife (in spite of her external behavior) is that she has decided, perhaps unconsciously, to use her strength as a substitute for his strong involvement with her. In effect she says, "I haven't received from you the strength or relationship for which I long, so I will be my own strength without you, even at the expense of the relationship I crave. It is too painful to yearn for what I cannot be guaranteed I will get from you." Her controlling spirit sabotages both at once: the loving involvement she desires from a strong man and the strength he wants to be able to give her. A wife's refusal to desire and expect strength from her husband reduces his stature as a man by increments.

This doesn't mean a woman should look for her husband to make up for her deficit of strength. Her identity grounded in Christ provides an inner integrity, whether her husband initiates on her behalf or not. But a wife is wrong to kill her longing that her husband bring his initiating strength to the relationship—a strength unlike her vigorous responsiveness, a strength that can be tender without capitulating to her. When a woman develops emotional independence by hardening herself against desiring her husband's involvement and protection, she damages her feminine soul.

A HUSBAND'S WRONG SPIRIT

A husband's spirit is also evident to his wife, regardless of his behavior and/or words. Though she may not be able to verbalize it, she knows when he is exercising his authority wrongly or for his self-protection rather than initiating strong and loving leadership with her good in mind.

Abusive Authority

A domineering man, for example, communicates to his wife his insecurity, and she knows in her spirit she is not strongly loved. If he is sometimes cruel or abusive, especially physically, her spirit will respond to him even in the good times with guardedness. The fear of being hurt runs deep, and a battered woman cannot rest comfortably in a marriage shadowed by her husband's unpredictability. The damage done by his anger sometimes leaves the relationship irreparable, even after one or both find help to reverse their destructive patterns.

Abdicated Authority

A passive husband also communicates his spirit without having to say a word. His wife knows when he is saying, "I don't want to be involved with you. You're frankly too much trouble." She senses his begrudging of the time and effort it takes to build a relationship, and her spirit receives his ongoing indifference with genuine, though often unacknowledged, pain. His withdrawal—or even his threat of withdrawal—from her emotionally, physically, sexually, or financially undermines her confidence in his love.

A passive husband's fearful or indecisive spirit delivers the message: "If I risk making this decision or taking this stand, I may fail. I would rather you take the responsibility so I'll be sure not to look bad." His refusal to act strongly on his wife's behalf engenders in her a sorrowful sense of loss for the security she should experience from his strong initiation.

CHANGE IN THE SPIRIT OF A MARRIAGE

If a husband and wife read each other's unspoken messages in their spirits, it is obvious that deep change in the relationship is impossible unless something changes in their spirits toward each other. External behavioral modifications will not suffice. What is required is not a Band-Aid for a minor cut but major surgery to excise the spiritual cancer. Not every marriage is terminally ill, of course, but whatever sunders the oneness of any marriage requires more than superficial attention.

In the final analysis, lasting marital change comes through the process of personal spiritual revival, which involves genuine repentance and confession of our failure to be good spouses at the deepest level of our marriages. We are bent toward wrong dependency as wives and abdication of authority as husbands, and apart from the Spirit's regenerating power, we cannot improve ourselves.

Roy Hession said in his preface to the 1973 edition of his book, *The Calvary Road,*

> revival is not a green valley getting greener, but a valley full of dry bones being made to live again and stand up an exceeding great army (Ezek. 37). It is not good Christians becoming better Christians—as God sees us there are not any good Christians—but rather Christians honestly confessing that their Christian life is a valley of dry bones and by that very confession qualifying for the grace that flows from the Cross and makes all things new.[1]

As spouses, we must acknowledge our wrong spirits and ask the Father to revive us by His Spirit; it is the only way to renewed life in our marriages.

My marital upheaval flowed unexpectedly from my prayer for personal spiritual revival. God always prompts relational changes (learning to love with His love) when He makes our hearts His home. Roy Hession reminds us, "It was into the home that sin first came. It is in the home that revival first needs to come. . . . It is the hardest place, the most costly, but the most necessary place to begin."[2] When God revives us personally, we will feel the impact in our marriages, not merely in surface adjustments but in deep spiritual renewal. Even if only one partner responds to the Spirit's reviving power, the marriage will be changed, and the other partner may be drawn to revitalized life in Christ.

A WIFE'S RIGHT SPIRIT

What, then, will characterize the inner spirit of a husband or wife committed to personal revival? According to the Apostle Peter, the gospel directly affects marriages. Addressing the spirit with which redeemed spouses ought to behave in their marriages, he wrote to women,

> Wives . . . be submissive to your husbands so that, if any of them do not believe the word, they may be won over without words by the behavior of their wives, when they see the purity and reverence of your lives. Your beauty should not come from outward adornment, such as braided hair and the wearing of gold jewelry and fine clothes. Instead, it should be that of your inner self, the unfading beauty of a gentle and quiet spirit, which is of great worth in God's sight. (1 Peter 3:1-4)

God is more interested in the renewed spirit of a woman than in her physical beauty, said Peter, referring to the distinguishing marks of the wealthy women of his day: hair elaborately braided with gold or silver (a deliberate show of opulence), costly jewelry, expensive clothing. The beauty that flows from a woman's "purity and reverence" is an inner spiritual reality that demands time and nurturing in her intimate and unhurried time with the Father. "Of great worth in God's sight" is a Christian woman's "unfading beauty of a gentle and quiet spirit." This responsiveness of spirit toward her husband's initiation is the essence of what Peter meant when he told wives to "be submissive to your husbands." What is distinctive about that kind of spirit?

A Gentle Spirit
Peter first called Christian wives to develop a gentle spirit. Some think that means they should be unassuming and remain in the background of their husbands' lives (and of the church's life), never asserting their opinions or offering their leadership. According to this view, a Christian woman dare not show any strength or competence lest she threaten or undermine her husband's headship. I have known many gifted women who pretended to be weak so they wouldn't intimidate their husbands or church leaders. Is it true that a godly woman cannot be

both strong and submissive (i.e., gentle)?

The Greek adjective *praos* (gentle) is also translated "meek," a word Jesus used to describe Himself (Matthew 11:29), and He was far from a weakling in any sense of the word. Rather, He was a man of steadfast strength, sure of Himself and of His calling. *Vine's Expository Dictionary of Old and New Testament Words* notes,

> The meekness manifested by the Lord and commended to the believer is the fruit of power. The common assumption is that when a man is meek it is because he cannot help himself; but the Lord was "meek" because He had the infinite resources of God at His command. Described negatively, meekness is the opposite to self-assertiveness and self-interest; it is equanimity of spirit that is neither elated nor cast down, simply because it is not occupied with self at all. (From *Notes on Galatians* by Hogg and Vine, pp. 294, 295.)[3]

A wife with a gentle spirit is not the stereotypical barometer wife, calculatedly helpless on the outside but hostile within. Rather, she possesses a confidence in her inner strength because she is connected to "the infinite resources of God." She is not weak or incompetent, nor does she pretend that she is. She uses her God-given giftedness not to advance her own position or to keep herself safe, but to serve others, especially her husband, according to their need.

A Quiet Spirit

Peter also called a woman to nurture the beauty of a quiet spirit, the opposite of the appeasement or antidependency of many wives. Some equate *quiet* with "silent" or "mousy," a woman who prefers to blend into the woodwork and say nothing. Actually, quietness has little to do with speaking, though Peter did exhort Christian wives married to unbelievers to win them "without words" by their godly lifestyle. But it is not in keeping silent that a woman evidences a quiet spirit. What she speaks, why she speaks, and how she speaks are far more important criteria.

"'Quiet' [the Greek word *hesuchios*] indicates tranquility arising from within, causing no disturbance to others."[4] Thus, quietness refers to a wife's spirit, not her tongue. A quiet woman possesses inner tranquility, does not need to prove herself to anyone, and is content to know her inner strength without using it to control someone else. She is the opposite of the woman who feels compelled to manage her circumstances or to change her husband's behavior so she can be happy. She has found God's peace by daily leaning on His love, and it flows from her into the lives of her husband and other family members. They know they can relax in her equanimity of spirit. Her words, when she speaks, will be for their good.

A Willing Spirit

Sometimes a woman caught in a difficult marriage may genuinely desire to submit to her husband, yet not be able to do so for one reason or another. Perhaps he absolutely refuses to take appropriate leadership or will not repent of a strong obsession with a particular temptation that hinders their relationship. Caught in this dilemma, a godly wife must first examine whether or not she has a *spirit* of submissiveness. She must ask herself if she is willing to drop her self-protection, risk being honest with him, practice letting go of her strategies for control- ling him, and express her desire to be submissive to him according to God's design—that is, she must develop a gentle and quiet spirit. She must not submit to her husband's habitual sin (cruelty, pornography, abuse, infidelity, alcoholism, etc.), but she must exhibit a willing spirit toward his leadership if and when he becomes willing to exercise it in a biblical way.

For example, if a man insists on maintaining an adulterous relationship, his wife must not submit to that decision. She is right to make him choose: Repent and give up the affair, or leave the marriage. If he genuinely repents and she forgives him, she must be willing to learn to trust and accept his leadership again (though it undoubtedly will require time and counseling to do so).

Or when a husband refuses to risk initiating leadership toward his wife even after she has told the truth and relinquished her control, she may have to accept the loss of a strong, loving man to whom she can respond. Yet she can choose not to harden herself against the pain his weakness causes her. She can refuse to look for a way to somehow get free or get even. She can accept the pain, draw her strength and wisdom from God, and learn to live with an imperfect man. God looks at her heart, at her spirit toward her husband, to discover whether or not she is genuinely *willing* to submit.

Ultimately, genuine submission is a chosen thing. The Greek verb *hupotasso*, translated "be submissive to" in Peter's first epistle and in Ephesians 5, is in the middle or passive voice, which means a wife's submission is what she does to herself. A wife chooses to place herself under her husband's recognized authority. He doesn't subject her; she subjects herself.

Jill Briscoe speculates that God might have said something like this to the "prime rib" He took from Adam with which He was planning to make Eve: "You will surely bring more joy to Adam as you yield and respond to him of your own glad will than you could as a mere piece of bone without the power of choice!"[5] Sometimes a husband demands submission—by making the consequences for nonsubmission unthinkably prohibitive, for example. But a husband who allows his wife the power of choice opens himself to receive her most precious gift— freely chosen submission to the man she loves.

A HUSBAND'S RIGHT SPIRIT

Peter addressed the choices a man makes about the spirit with which he approaches his wife. A husband must initiate strong involvement with his wife, neither ignoring nor abusing her. Peter wrote,

> Husbands, in the same way be considerate as you live with your wives, and treat them with respect as the weaker partner and as heirs with you of the gracious gift of life, so that nothing will hinder your prayers. (1 Peter 3:7)

A Considerate Spirit

First of all, a husband's spirit is to be one of loving initiation and consideration, the opposite of passivity. This does not mean simply that a man should treat his wife with courtesy, though that is involved, too. The *King James Version* translates the opening phrase this way: "Likewise, ye husbands, dwell with them according to knowledge." The Greek word for knowledge (*gnosis*) means "primarily a seeking to know, an enquiry, investigation."[6] Thus, what is implied is that a husband ought to aggressively investigate his wife's likes, dislikes, strengths, weaknesses, and moods, know what she is like, and take that into consideration in his involvement with her. His spirit must demonstrate his attempts to see things from her point of view and to understand who she is. A woman knows when she is being genuinely heard rather than tolerated. Her husband's spirit will communicate it to her spirit, despite his words or actions to the contrary.

An Esteeming Spirit

Peter goes on to admonish Christian husbands to manifest a spirit of genuine respect toward their wives, to give them from their hearts a place of honor (the opposite of dominating or abusing them). A man's spirit toward his wife ought to convince her that he thinks her special and desires to show her admiration. He must also insist on that esteem toward her from others, especially their children.

If she does not merit his admiration because her heart is turned against him or God, he must be willing to confront her in love and do what he can to woo her back to a place of honor (as Hosea did for Gomer to model God's love for His people [Hosea 1–3]). A woman instinctively knows whether or not her husband's words and actions flow from a heart that values and esteems her, and his respect, if it is genuine and ungrudging, is a source of strength to her.

Peter adds two clarifications regarding men's respect for their wives. First, he reminds husbands that their mates are the "weaker partner," a phrase eliciting considerable controversy in the interpretation of this passage. Surely Peter cannot have meant that wives are morally or spiritually weak in comparison to their husbands; that would violate the message and examples of the rest of Scripture. Many commentators think Peter is referring to the greater physical weakness of women, and that explanation has some validity.

But in the context of his passage, it seems to me Peter is encouraging husbands to remember that their wives are in a "weaker" position as far as their place in the authority-submission relationship, which he has been advocating as God's design for marriage. A wife was in a weaker place than her husband legally and culturally in that day. Then (as now) she needed his initiation as leader to support, guide, and encourage her life. Peter's comment about a wife's "weakness" was intended to make her husband respect her more, not less, drawing him to protect and cherish her as the responder to his loving leadership.

Second, Peter counsels husbands that treating their Christian wives with respect means remembering that they are "heirs with [them] of the gracious gift of life." In other words, their wives are as saved and as spiritually endowed as they are. As Paul says elsewhere, when it comes to equality of spiritual blessings, "there is neither Jew nor Greek, slave nor free, male nor female, for you are all one in Christ Jesus" (Galatians 3:28).

It is significant that Peter forbids any inferiority-superiority spiritual distinctions between men and women (they are equally heirs) while at the same time he insists on the authority-submission functional distinction in marriage (submit and be considerate). Husbands and wives are equal inheritors of God's wonderful grace through Jesus, but they are called to live out their redemption by observing their differing marital responsibilities as leaders and responders.

UNHINDERED SPIRITUAL FELLOWSHIP

Peter closes by warning husbands and wives to obey his instructions "so that nothing will hinder your prayers" (1 Peter 3:7). It is a reminder that a couple's oneness or division happens in the spirit, and observing God's pattern for marital relationship affects both partners' intimacy with God as well. One's prayers, the lifeline to the Father, can be interrupted by brokenness in marriage. The NIV Study Bible concludes, "Spiritual fellowship, with God and with one another, may be hindered by disregarding God's instruction concerning husband-wife relationships."[7] Who we are to each other has an impact on who we are to God.

SUMMING UP

Our culture, even our Christian culture, predisposes us to judge according to the obvious. We tend to evaluate by what can be seen and measured rather than by what is intuitively or spiritually discerned. God's way of judging, however, is precisely the opposite. The integrity of one's spirit or heart is the measure by which He appraises that person's life (1 Samuel 16:7). So also with one's marriage; it wilts or thrives in its spirit, not in its externals. If a marriage is to genuinely flourish, not just survive, both partners must nurture spiritual dependence on God as the wellspring of life. That is the topic of the next chapter.

NOTES:
1. Roy and Revel Hession, *The Calvary Road* (Fort Washington, Pa.: Christian Literature Crusade, 1988), page 12.
2. Hession, page 70.
3. W.E. Vine, "meek," *Vine's Expository Dictionary of Old and New Testament Words,* vol. 3 (Old Tappan, N.J.: Fleming H. Revell, 1981), page 56.
4. Vine, "quiet," vol. 3, page 242.
5. Jill Briscoe, *Prime Rib and Apple* (Grand Rapids: The Zondervan Corporation, 1976), page 16.
6. Vine, "knowledge," vol. 2, page 301.
7. *The NIV Study Bible,* Kenneth Barker ed. (Grand Rapids: Zondervan Bible Publishers, 1985), page 1892.

QUESTIONS FOR THOUGHT AND DISCUSSION

1. What can you say about how a wife's antidependent spirit makes her husband feel?

2. In what ways was Jesus' spirit different from the antidependent spirit or hostile dependency of many wives? (See John 4:34, 6:38; and Hebrews 12:2.)

3. What effect do you think a husband's retreating spirit (either passive or abusive) has on his wife?

4. Explain how Jesus' love for His Church is neither abusive (retreating from love) nor passive (retreating from involvement and honest confrontation).
     Revelation 2:1-3
     Revelation 2:4-6

5. How does a wife's chosen submission reflect the spirit of Jesus toward His Father? (See Philippians 2:5-8.)

6. Indicate how a husband's esteeming spirit toward his wife reflects the spirit of Jesus toward His Church. (See Ephesians 5:25-27 and Revelation 2:19.)

13

GOD-DEPENDENCE:
The Threshold to Freedom

If the health of a marriage is determined by the spiritual intimacy of its partners with each other based on their spiritual revival process, many Christian spouses must grapple with some serious questions. What if one person wants to change and the other does not? What if the change process produces distancing instead of healing? How does one give up control without giving up hope? And what do we do with the pain of disappointment when we deeply realize things will never be as perfect as we wish?

The answer lies ultimately in one's experience of spiritual intimacy with God—not just attending church and having devotions (though these activities are important), but nurturing an ongoing, honest *relationship* with the Father. At its core will be repentance (looking for ways one is failing to love), a glad receiving of grace, and a conscious movement toward abandoning self-protective strategies in one's relationships with others.

When either or both spouses commit themselves to removing the masks behind which they have been hiding, they must also bond more and more with the Father. Throughout the process of my marital mask-dropping, I experienced that my downward spiral in terms of pain (facing ever deeper disappointments in my relationship with Bill) corresponded to my upward spiral in terms of dependency on God (experiencing more frequently that my inner life was secure in the Father's love). It was not that I needed Bill less and less (he would have been rightly jealous of God if I had used that strategy), but that I came to depend on the Father in the midst of my marital pain. As spouses practice living without masks with each other, they must also live without masks before the Father.

Freedom from pretense in the marriage relationship is never free. Its cost is brokenness before God and total submission of our wills to His. There is no cheap grace, and there is also no cheap submission to the Father. We hate being dependent; our very nature militates against it. We are deeply and sinfully committed to spiritual independence. We want to dig our own wells (Jeremiah 2:13) and light our own torches (Isaiah 50:10-11) instead of seeking the Fountain of living water to quench our thirst and the Light of the world to illuminate our dark places.

Our lack of faith in God's love has stubborn roots in our pride and self-sufficiency. We just do not want to have to depend on Him completely. We would much rather stay in charge, plan for the future, hedge all our bets, keep life predictable (even if painful), and know ahead of time how we are going to handle any worst-case scenario. Mentally, we know God is adequate, but we feel safer relying on ourselves.

JESUS' DEPENDENCE

We don't really want to live like Jesus lived, even though He promised that would bring genuine rest to our souls (Matthew 11:29). He lived unattached to this world's "treasures," listening to His Father's voice instead of the voices around Him, and He moved toward others in love and forgiveness despite their rejection, misunderstanding, and betrayal. Though we cannot duplicate Jesus' perfect obedience, we can seek the life He promised by imitating His dependence on the Father, which sustained Him throughout the pain.

Jesus utterly depended on the Father, and He calls us to do the same—personally and in our marriages—even though there will be pain in the process. Not until we're Home will our longings for intimacy be fully satisfied in His presence. We want relief from pain and the satisfaction of our desires *now*, and sometimes God gives us tastes of that in our marriages and in our intimate moments with Him. But we are wrong to think abundant life is attainable without the pain of sacrifice—the relinquishment of self-reliance, which leads to greater dependence on and intimacy with the Father.

Inner spiritual strength grows only in the soil of brokenness, which God alone can revitalize. Without that kind of inner strength, we will be frustrated time after time with our feeble attempts, as wives, to submit to or, as husbands, to sacrificially love the spouses whose flaws we know most intimately.

A WIFE'S DEPENDENCE ON GOD

For a woman to genuinely and lastingly submit to her husband, she must first submit her will in brokenness to the Father. Paul instructed wives to "submit to your husbands as to the Lord" (Ephesians 5:22), which assumes they have given themselves to the headship of Christ. A Christian wife must learn from Jesus' example to abandon herself in trust of the Father's leading (as Jesus "entrusted himself to him who judges justly" during His suffering [1 Peter 2:21-23]). Jesus knew He was God, yet He humbled Himself unto death (Philippians 2:5-7), thus modeling for Christian wives in every age genuine submission from a position of strength. A Christian wife can know herself strong with the dignity of her identity in Christ and, in that strength (through her weakness), submit herself to what her husband needs by dropping her self-protection for his sake.

No woman can risk exposure to and rejection from her husband, giving him that edge of emotional power over her, without increasingly trusting in God's love and acceptance of her. And if she turns her dependence away from her husband but not toward God, investing her emotional portfolio in children or work, in a close friend or a lover, her dependence will remain death-bound. She may find someone more worthy of her love or more pleasant circumstances or a degree of equanimity in unpleasant circumstances. But she will miss God's best: an intimacy with the Father out of which to draw the resources for loving strongly and vulnerably the person to whom she is covenantally bound.

A HUSBAND'S DEPENDENCE ON GOD

For a man to increasingly drop his self-protection and involve himself with the one to whom he has bound himself by covenant, he must also continually submit his will in brokenness to the Father. When a husband is under the pressure of learning to initiate *agape* love toward an imperfect wife, he will have to depend utterly on God for the power to do so. Especially if she does not respond to his more assertive leadership or gentler love, he will need the Father's unconditional acceptance and encouragement to keep on keeping on.

Jesus provided for all husbands a model for sacrificial giving through absolute dependence on His Father as He laid down His life for His Bride, the Church. Jesus said, "I tell you the truth, the Son can do nothing by himself; he can do only what he sees his Father doing, because whatever the Father does the Son also does" (John 5:19). In submission to His Father's will, Jesus laid down His life for His own.

POWER TO LIVE IN DEPENDENCE

But it is not just that Jesus provided us an example of how to submit and love. More than that, through the Spirit He gives us the freedom and power to do so. When we as marriage partners rely on God's unconditional acceptance of us, we can face our peculiar styles of protecting ourselves and have the courage to repent of them and drop them. A husband can give his wife more of what she needs (his strength, involvement, protection, and leadership) because the Father is equipping him from His endless adequacy. And a wife can give her husband more of what he needs (herself, her softness, her responsive dependence on him as a strong man) because the Father is supplying her with His infinite love. If we know ourselves adequate and loved, we can risk being perceived as inadequate or unlovely by our mates. It will hurt, but we can continue to risk loving each other in God's strength.

Thus, a wife's biblical submission and a husband's loving leadership must be rooted in their relationship with God. She can know herself loved to be free to submit, and he can know himself strong to be free to love. And both can know genuine freedom from the pressure to procure their love and/or adequacy from each other because of their relationship with God through Christ.

Dependence on God doesn't free us from pain. In fact, we will probably experience more pain as we face our unmet longings for perfect love and discover how even our tastes of intimacy with God can never fully satisfy this side of Home. In one of my journal entries I wrote,

> God is enough, but that doesn't alleviate the pain; He doesn't *feel* like enough. Yet sometimes in bright snatches of intimacy with Him (though more often in a quiet and unobtrusive way), a certain knowledge is beginning to grow, a sureness that whether He removes the pain in this marriage or not, whether I *feel* like He's enough or not, He has become my sufficiency. It's not perceived directly, but in side glances, or reflected in a mirror out of the corner of the eye—the inner knowledge that life without Him is unthinkable, that having Him plus the pain is infinitely better than being without both. His presence doesn't undo nor even diminish the pain. It is more like the framework for it, the backdrop against which it's possible to let myself feel the hurt and the sadness.

The Father's love doesn't abolish pain (it didn't for Jesus, either), but His presence does make it bearable.

UNEVEN SPIRITUAL GROWTH BETWEEN PARTNERS

Finally, we must go back to a difficult question: What if one marriage partner is connected to the power and grace of God (i.e., is born again) and the other is not? Beyond that concern, what about unequal yoking in a Christian marriage, one partner longing for maturity and the other indifferent or resistant? It is a significant problem in the Church today, especially because most unequal marriages involve a growing wife and a disinterested husband, and the wife's submission to her husband in such cases becomes an excruciating task. Not only is she bereft spiritually, but she is also losing the blessing that should be hers of responding to her husband's spiritual leadership. How can she submit to him spiritually if he is spiritually dormant? What will happen if she pursues her spiritual nurturing and leaves her husband "in the dust"? Is that even a godly choice?

Relinquishing the Dream

Two New Testament passages seem to deal most directly with this quandary. Peter addressed the problem when he admonished Christian women to submit to their pagan husbands "so that, if any of them do not believe the word, they may be won over without words by the behavior of their wives, when they see the purity and reverence of [their] lives" (1 Peter 3:1-2). Many Christian women whose husbands are disinterested in spiritual growth endeavor to ease the pain of their unequal yoking by trying to shore up their husbands' spirituality. They give them books, invite them to seminars, introduce them to other Christian men, and try to spiritualize their conversations whenever they can. I know one woman who used her prayer time with her husband to tell God aloud what she thought he ought to be like.

Peter instructed the wife (or husband) caught in an unequal spiritual relationship: Pursue wordlessly your walk with the Father, and let your spouse be drawn (if God intends to draw him or her) by your inner transformation through the Spirit's sanctifying work. Give up the dream of remaking your partner into a more spiritually responsive person. Leave that to God.

Of course, dreams never die painlessly. A man or woman alive in Christ desires more than anything to share that life in the intimacy of marriage, and he or she experiences deep loneliness of spirit with a spiritually listless spouse. Sometimes what keeps the marriage going is the hope that revival will someday happen and infuse the relationship with new vibrancy and oneness.

Allowing that hope to die and facing the vacuum of spiritual fellowship in the marriage will require great courage and increasing dependence on the Father's comfort in the midst of penetrating sorrow. God has promised that suffering yielded to His sovereignty will produce both spiritual maturity (Romans 5:3-5, James 1:2-4, 1 Peter 1:6-7) and eventual reward (Romans 8:17-18).

Pursuing Spiritual Integrity

Paul addressed a similar problem when he wrote this to the Corinthian Christians whose spouses were not believers:

> If any brother has a wife who is not a believer and she is willing to live with him, he must not divorce her. And if a woman has a

husband who is not a believer and he is willing to live with her, she must not divorce him. . . . But if the unbeliever leaves, let him do so. A believing man or woman is not bound in such circumstances; God has called us to live in peace. How do you know, wife, whether you will save your husband? Or, how do you know, husband, whether you will save your wife? (1 Corinthians 7:12-13,15-16)

This passage implies that a believer must pursue a relationship with God and grow in grace regardless of the spiritual state of the marriage partner. Unequal yoking is not a legitimate reason for divorce, but neither is it a reason not to grow spiritually. Holding back in one's spiritual walk to avoid inequality of spiritual communion violates the principle Paul asserted: "If the unbeliever leaves, let him do so." Believers are called to go on even if alone, to follow Jesus at any cost, but without abandoning the responsibility to love one's mate as oneself. If distancing happens (and it certainly will), the growing Christian must accept the resulting loneliness as part of the price for following God.

One effect of this distancing is the serious imbalance of the submission-authority aspect of the marital relationship. In what areas, for example, must a Christian wife submit to her unsaved or spiritually immature husband, and how does a Christian man spiritually lead his unbelieving or indifferent wife? There are no easy answers that will apply in every marriage. But the guidelines are these: the believing spouse must seek to more closely follow after God, more consistently drop his or her self-protection, and more genuinely minister to the other's needs. As we seek to live redeemed lives in a fallen world with fallen mates, we must learn to speak the truth in love and let go of our control-retreat strategies. We must trust the Father to forgive our failures to love for the sake of His Son and trust the Spirit to encourage, strengthen, and instruct us daily.

HOPE FOR SPIRITUAL ONENESS

It is possible (but not guaranteed) that despite initial distancing, eventually the sanctification of one partner may entice the other into similar growth: "How do you know, wife, whether you will save your husband? Or, how do you know, husband, whether you will save your wife?" A Christian spouse increasingly committed to genuine love and honest confrontation (but not condemnation) through the power of the Holy Spirit is very attractive. True revival reproduces the very beauty of Jesus in a believer's inner life, and Jesus draws irresistibly those His Father has chosen (John 6:44,65). Often God touches the spirit of the uncommitted partner so that he or she also begins a more vigorous pursuit of God.

That, of course, brings up another issue. Though an immature Christian's renewal brings joy to the more mature partner, what about the gap of spiritual experience between them? Can there be spiritual oneness?

The answer lies in the nature of spiritual fellowship. In contrast to other kinds of fellowship (intellectual, for example), which demand a certain equality of experience or growth to be enjoyed, spiritual oneness between Christians happens whenever two people indwelt by the same Holy Spirit share their blessings in Christ. One may know more than the other about the ways of God with His beloved, but both know the wonderful joy of being beloved. A spouse who has just begun to grow can enjoy genuine spiritual fellowship with his or her mature believing spouse because their hearts are knit together in friendship with Jesus.

Moreover, if an immature believer and a mature believer come to God together, their walk with each other will be increasingly close. Each will have something to learn and give because both will be receiving particular gifts from the Father's hand. The "young" believer can sometimes teach the "old" believer, even though the latter may have greater Bible knowledge. Knowledge is not the point (though both should pursue it). Oneness flows not from equality of knowledge, but from a shared relationship with God.

Thus, even if the husband is the less mature spouse, if he begins and continues to walk in intimate fellowship with the Father, he can more often serve as the spiritual leader or initiator in the relationship. It may take time for him to develop confidence in this role, and the more spiritually mature wife must remain willing and eager for him to do so.

He must pursue his study of the Word and develop relationships with other Christian men in order to build his spiritual life, not looking to his wife as his primary source of spiritual information. He will take from her shoulders the pressure to be his spiritual adviser and will free her to share whatever insights she may have as an adjunct to (rather than the source of) his spiritual growth. Redemption of such a marriage to its biblical balance of the husband as spiritual leader is most certainly possible through God's sanctifying power.

DANGERS OF SPIRITUAL UNEVENNESS

Accelerated spiritual growth by one partner has the potential not only to draw the other partner (if his or her heart is open to God), but also to repel the other partner (if his or her heart is hardened against God). This is precisely why many godly men and women don't relentlessly pursue God. They fear losing what little spiritual intimacy they have with their mates, which is a formidable risk.

God intended spiritual oneness in marriage as the bedrock on which all other oneness is built, and it is tragic when a Christian must choose between intimacy with God or intimacy with his or her mate. Fear of spiritual sundering keeps many believing spouses in spiritual infancy for fear of growing up and outdistancing the spiritual walk of their partners altogether.

Perhaps a spouse's going on alone with God reflects one aspect of the sacrifice Jesus spoke of when He declared, "If anyone comes to me and does not hate his father and mother, his wife and children, his brothers and sisters—yes, even his own life—he cannot be my disciple" (Luke 14:26). This hatred refers to choosing relationship with God over any other human relationship. When a man or woman hears God's call, he or she must put everything else in second place, but without ever abandoning God's mandate to love others selflessly. In a marriage, that means a believing husband or wife will be committed to spiritual growth with God but will also be committed to the relentless pursuit of loving his or her partner as undemandingly and unself-protectively as possible.

It's lonely going on alone spiritually. Paradoxically, however, embracing the pain of that loneliness instead of running from it will disarm its power so we are no longer controlled by its specter. When I abandoned myself to God, the spiritual loneliness in my marriage intensified, and I was in a lot of pain. But the loneliness didn't destroy me because my life was hidden more and more in Christ. In fact, it eventually deepened my love for Bill, a love born of pain but increasingly independent of his response. God intended that I learn to love Bill with Jesus' kind of suffering passion, which could flourish even in the absence of reciprocal love. Although the loneliness hurt, it lost its power to dictate my choices.

Sometimes, the spiritual revival of one spouse reveals the spiritual deadness of the other. When light discloses the sin of darkness, repentance is demanded. If the uncommitted partner refuses to repent, preferring darkness over light, he or she may leave the marriage rather than live with the discomfort of such close proximity to light. The tragedy of divorce sometimes follows on the heels of renewed spiritual vitality by one spouse. Paul may have been thinking of this when he taught, "If the unbeliever leaves, let him do so" (1 Corinthians 7:15). A man or woman committed to following God at any cost, willing to unconditionally minister to his or her mate with genuine love, may experience in spite of the best efforts the death of an unequal marriage. When pursuing God, one must hold up even one's marriage in upturned palms, trusting the loving Sovereign Father to work all things for good.

SUMMING UP

None of this movement into spiritual dependence on God alone will happen without personal cost. Freedom to submit and freedom to love are paid for by the intentional sacrifice of our dearest dreams on the altar of obedience to the Father's will. Even as we abandon ourselves to God and find our life in Him, we will know pain in our marital relationship because every human relationship will somehow disappoint us. Even our hunger for God will not be fully satisfied until we are Home.

If we battle our dependence on God, run from our loneliness, and demand that God's loving presence be uninterrupted by the pressures of daily living, we will never know true freedom. Christian maturity requires that we dwell in a broken world without complaint, embracing our pain, abiding in Jesus, depending utterly on the Spirit, loving those the Father gives us to love, and yearning for the joy of our eventual Homecoming. That is what it means to live free in our marriages. It is a costly freedom, but worth the price.

QUESTIONS FOR THOUGHT AND DISCUSSION

1. Name the things in your circumstances that make it hard (or "unnecessary") for you to live in dependence on God.

2. What in your nature or background makes dependence on God difficult for you?

3. Read the passages listed below. Explain what each says about the necessity of brokenness and absolute dependence on God.
    Psalm 51:17
    Jeremiah 29:12-13
    John 3:36
    John 15:5
    James 4:7-10
    1 John 5:12

4. According to 2 Corinthians 5:17, how is it possible for us to consider ourselves *already* loved (as wives) and *already* strong (as husbands) in our marriages?

5. In what way is it freeing for us as wives and as husbands to know ourselves already loved or already strong in our marriages?

14

BEYOND COPING:
Integrity Through Process

Learning to live free in our marriages without the masks of false submission or inappropriate authority goes beyond merely coping with certain difficult realities of our lives. God wants to thrust us into spiritual revival in our personal and marital lives, to show us our disappointments and our sin so that we can cry out, confess, and find rest in His forgiveness. He would have us live in the terror of grace, growing in the confidence of being loved and equipped by Him, and from that position of strength (not deficit) learn to love each other with *agape* love.

It is a noble and worthy task to which we have been called by the Sovereign God of the universe, but we cannot accomplish it overnight. What He calls us to is not an event (though it may begin with an event) but a process. It is a process of change and growth that will exhilarate and terrify and profoundly disturb us for years to come. In short, He has called us to live life, and to live it unmasked.

The accomplishment of our God-ordained task requires three things. First, we must commit ourselves to several particulars in the change process. We also should know what to expect as we embark on our journey into coming fully alive. And we must be willing to wait, to

183

accept the ups and downs of being in process without having yet "arrived." Let's examine each requisite for living without our masks.

GENUINE COMMITMENT

One requisite for freedom is that we make several commitments. First, we must be committed to the marriage itself. Spouses who take lightly their sacred covenantal vows lack incentive to engage in the arduous process of abandoning their unique styles of self-protection and of learning to love each other in the right way. It is remarkably easy in today's culture for two fallen people to avoid pushing past the pain threshold in their relationship to reach the goal of true intimacy.

Many couples (even Christian couples) simply give up on their marriages, and frequently each partner repeats the protective strategies with someone new. But those who find themselves bound by their vows to a disappointing marriage don't have to be married and miserable. Through the inner freedom Christ provides, they can remain married without being miserable. However, the process will be excruciating, and their commitment to the marriage will be essential.

Second, we must commit ourselves to risking. The restraints of our lives—the boundaries within which God has placed us—are unique to our particular situations, so the risks we take will be unique for every person and every couple. But unless we jump time and again from our comfortable cliffs of safety, telling the truth in love and removing our claws of control or retreat, we will never know the strong love God offers those who seek Him with all their hearts. We must, in short, live dangerously in the personal and spiritual arenas of our lives. We must look to God to preserve our inner lives, even (maybe especially) when our circumstances suggest we are fools to do so.

In our risking, we must trust and obey God's Spirit in us and devour God's Word as though it was vital to our survival, because it is. In fact, commitment to risking in our marriages demands that our dependence on God preempt all competing hungers and all potential distractions. God must become the only source of our inner lives as we risk strongly loving our mates.

Finally, we must commit ourselves to asking for help from others during our growth process. Jesus' raising of Lazarus from the dead (John 11:38-44) illustrates the coming of revival into our marriages.

Just as Lazarus could not have given new life to himself, so must our new life come from Jesus into the cavern of our death and resurrect us. Nor could Lazarus have sustained his renewed life by himself. When he emerged from his tomb, he was bound by grave clothes—linen strips wrapped mummylike around his body and layered with aromatic spices. Jesus turned to Lazarus's sisters and friends and said, "Take off the grave clothes and let him go" (John 11:44). Like Lazarus, we cannot unbind ourselves. Our process of spiritual growth and marital healing involves human agents who will help unwrap from our souls the grave clothes of shameful self-images, putrifying habits of self-protection, and rotting patterns of bitterness and unrepentance. We must admit that we need others if we are to learn to love, though our self-reliance screams in protest. Life in community has always been God's design for His Church.

My ongoing process would have been impossible without a Christian support community whose wisdom and love during our regular times together still help me see what I cannot see by myself. Not only do they at times preserve my sanity, they also stretch my faith, encouraging, confronting, and praying for me. More than that, they provide me with the opportunity to learn to love appropriately as together we practice being honest and open.

But they cannot be everything to me, nor should they take Bill's place in my life. Once I went to a group meeting when I was angry with Bill, and I wanted to dominate the entire evening by talking about my problems. Knowing how demanding that would be, I waited until after the meeting to voice my frustration, but then only one person listened. That made me doubly angry—with Bill and with my friends. No one was available to hear me. So I decided to avoid the group party scheduled for later that week. I couldn't spoil everyone's good time by sharing my pain, and I couldn't just ignore how bad I felt. Besides, I wanted to punish them for letting me down.

Then the Father reminded me that no human relationship can ever provide the perfect love I was built to receive. More than that, He showed me my sin of unlove, of wanting to use my friends for myself instead of reaching out to love them. Later I wrote in my journal,

I still don't know the first thing about loving right. The deeper I go into pain, the more I use people to assuage my grief, trying to balance out the loss of Bill's love with the gain of my friends' consolation. And I can't fix my selfish unlove toward them. I can't just choose not to hurt, nor can I genuinely love them when I'm in so much pain—I have nothing to give. My only recourse (other than revenge or avoidance or getting new friends to make *them* do for me) is to repent—to simply look honestly at the depth of my unlove and agree with the Father that my heart is desperately selfish and that forgiveness through the Blood is my only hope.

My confession cleansed me anew, as it always does. Though it didn't alleviate the pain, I could finally choose to stay alone in my pain, telling it to the One who hears. I went to the party after all, and the Father graced me not to demand center stage but to give of myself to hear my friends' joy and pain because He was there for me and He was enough. I also received gratefully what they could give me (and it was a lot, because they are real and they really do love me) without holding them responsible for my happiness. Inch by labored inch, the Father is teaching me to receive His love so I can begin to love my neighbor as myself. My support community is absolutely vital to my spiritual maturing.

So many Christians remain like the newly resurrected Lazarus, bound in stinking remnants of the past because they refuse to admit they cannot unwrap themselves from their spiritual and emotional garments of death. We must get past our horror of being unmasked in the presence of fellow believers—and perhaps a professional Christian counselor as well—and agree to become accountable for our continued progress, guided by others' perceptions of how we are doing. It is the only way we can learn to walk free.

REALISTIC EXPECTATIONS

It is also important to know what to expect from our venture into the unknown of our healing process. Of course, no two recovery processes will be alike, but we can reliably anticipate some general characteristics. For one thing, the first partner to drop his or her mask (and the process is seldom begun simultaneously) will likely encounter an angry resistance to what is happening. People avoid change until they have no other choice, and when one begins the process, the other will most likely demand a return to the status quo.

Concurrent with the resistance will come deep disruption in the marriage. Nothing will be the same. Both partners must expect the unexpected, expect confusion, expect to be in limbo. Getting well is a messy business with unpredictability as its hallmark. Instead of everything falling into place, everything usually falls apart. Sometimes for months at a time, the internal discomfort of new honesty and unmasked pain will combine with the tumultuous disquiet of relational unevenness, and life will seem utterly out of control.

During those times, everything in us will want to regain control and do something—anything—to bring order to the chaos and equanimity to the relationship. But someone once said, "If you're not making waves, you're not under way." Growth always causes emotional disquietude, which in turn exerts pressure on both partners to resort to their former self-protective strategies. Pressing on toward renewed honesty and risking at those times of inner stress are essential if the marriage is to become all it can be.

Another thing we must face as a normal part of the growth process is the inevitability of pain and loneliness. Even with the undergirding of a support group, spiritual brokenness and renewal are intensely personal and private. The process of marital change and healing is a lonely journey, even though the potential for intimacy and spiritual fellowship may be a legitimate hope. One of my journal entries reads, "I am carrying the weight of a waiting love. My dear one is fighting his own inner war and I am alien to his pain. He is not deliberately shutting me out, but I am outside nonetheless and I am lonely, not a railing or an angry loneliness, but a quiet and sad and waiting thing." We must learn to love with Jesus' kind of suffering love, which means we can expect to be hurt and to be lonely.

Finally, we must expect mistakes. Living in a fallen world assumes relapses in our growth process, but our high expectations in the marital arena, often prevent us from accepting our own or our spouses' imperfections. If we would learn to live free, we must learn to sometimes allow ourselves to fail and also to accept our partners' failures as well. God loves us where we are (though He's not content to let us stay there), and that is how we must learn to love ourselves and each other, too.

PATIENT PERSEVERANCE

We must remember that the process of marital recovery to a biblical balance of submission and authority is just that: a process. There are no quick cures or clearly defined steps to follow as we learn to speak the truth and let go of our control or retreat strategies. Whenever we perceive a clear leading of the Spirit to do or refrain from doing something in relationship to our spouses, we are responsible for doing it, and the sooner the better. But the calisthenics of healing cannot be reduced to a neat little program applicable to all marriages, nor can they be done in isolation from each other. We are in process, and we must be willing to wait—sometimes for years—while that process works itself out.

One of our problems is that habits have memories. Sometimes a couple have for years made marital decisions based on self-protective strategies, and deeply ingrained habits don't go away just because spouses gain insight into their behavior. Like teeth that without retainers move back to their preorthadontic positions when the braces come off, our old relational patterns automatically take over without continual vigilance and consciously made new decisions. Steve Brown, my pastor, says about Christ's victory over Satan, "The dragon is dead, but his tail still swishes." We must be patient with ourselves and our spouses during the extended time necessary for replacing old habits with new healthy ones.

Though there will be times of stress and heartbreaking loneliness during our changing years, we must also learn to relax in the hands of a loving God who knows what He intends for us and knows it is good. Like a patient lover, He is persistent (even relentless) in His pursuit of re-creation in our lives, but He is never pushy. We are impatient to be finished, perfected, whole, but God takes His time, knowing the stages and orchestrating the events that will take us step by step into His plan for our healing. We want to sprint, but God wants us to put one foot in front of the other. He perceives that we cannot bypass any of the stages (like the anger or heartache or sadness or fear).

The Father has promised beauty for ashes in His own time (perhaps not until we're Home), and we can learn to trust His workmanship. Someone once said God is never in a hurry, nor is He ever late. A palace is built a brick at a time, and God is both architect and builder of the monument He is creating to His glory out of the rubble of our brokenness before Him. Our timetable for the completion of that monument is almost never the same as His, but we must learn to believe that His is better.

In the meantime, we must also learn to enjoy whatever we can with gladness. When our spouses do reach out to us to speak to our hearts (at whatever level they are able to do so), we must practice receiving and enjoying it without anxiety (that it will not last) or anger (that it is not as much as we want or need). I once wrote in my journal, "I am beginning to be able to savor Bill's love without devouring it, to enjoy it without being consumed by needing more." We must look for ways to find beauty in our world and fellowship with our friends, to see God's good gifts even through our tears. We must celebrate life and offer our love whenever we can, learning to be content with the less-than-ideal.

In the process of change and growth in our marriages, God is at work remaking each of us. He may not change our circumstances, but He will surely change us. He uses our circumstances to conform us (as was His stated intention) into the likeness of His Son (Romans 8:28-29).

Sometimes the only thing we feel is the sandpaper of His finishing work on our character, and it is all we can do to choose not to run from the pain. But when He stops sanding for a time, we can enjoy the respite and in the quiet hear His approval of our yieldedness to His craftsmanship. We can open ourselves to joy as well as sorrow. We can learn to laugh—not the laughter of cynicism at the pain we have known, but the laughter of joy at becoming through the pain the free men and women He has created us to be, individually and in our marriages. Far beyond coping, we can both enjoy and anticipate the freedom and integrity of living without our masks.

SUMMING UP

When a husband or wife is faced with the overwhelming task of learning to love an imperfect mate God's way, he or she is inclined to ask: Why do it at all? Why go through the pain and hard work of learning to face loneliness and heartache and to biblically submit or sacrificially love from the heart? Why even stay in a marriage that offers so much less than might be possible with someone else?

Why indeed? If happiness is the goal, separation and divorce are sometimes eminently advisable. But if Christlikeness is the goal, what is needed is not release from our unhappy marriages but release from the inner bondage that keeps us unhappy in our marriages. There have been times when both Bill and I wanted out of our marriage, but the Father wouldn't say yes. It wasn't because God intended to make it a success story (there are no success-story marriages, only keep-working-at-it marriages). It was because He wanted us to learn to live free—not free *from* each other but free *with* each other. We are freed in Christ to love God's way, no strings attached.

I thought the process would kill me, but what is dying is what has to die—my chronic fear of abandonment, my desperate need to control, my congenital failure to love. What has survived is my intimacy with the Father and my love for Bill, an eyes-open love that can see the worst and not run away, a love that no longer needs rose-colored glasses to keep me reaching out to him.

Surely our culture offers many simpler and more enjoyable alternatives for dealing with the emptiness and pain we often experience in our marital relationships. But in our spirits we know there are some things more heart-satisfying than merely avoiding pain. We sense we were built for Heaven, and we instinctively know nothing will satisfy but God Himself. In our honest moments we recognize that easy answers and quick fixes are not enough. We have to have the real thing, whatever the cost.

When God draws us to Himself with the loveliness of His grace, our revival to new life awakens within us an unquenchable desire to return His love and to love others the way He loves us, especially in the intimacy of our marriages. Left to love on our own ability, we would be doomed from the start. We cannot love in our own strength. But redeemed and given a taste of God's unconditional love, we both want and are enabled through the Spirit to love with that same powerful love. Once we know how it feels to be alive, we cannot go back to merely existing.

Aliveness has a price tag. When we open ourselves to joy, we also open ourselves to suffering and a deep sense of transience in this world. The writer of the book of Hebrews commended the Old Testament patriarchs for "still living by faith when they died. They did not receive the things promised; they only saw them and welcomed them from a distance. And they admitted that they were aliens and strangers on earth . . . longing for a better country—a heavenly one" (Hebrews 11:13,16).

And so it is with us (though unlike them, we have seen many of those promises fulfilled in Jesus). As committed as we must be to our marriages, our spouses, and our individual spiritual processes, we must remember that in the final analysis, we are destined for life in a different dimension altogether. Being built for Heaven means that as our spiritual life with God deepens and we come to know the sweetness of intimacy with Him, we will experience a relentless ache underlying all of life, a longing for reality that cannot be fully satisfied until we are Home. Our yearning will be exquisitely intense when we are in pain, but it will infuse even the best of times with a bittersweet hunger for eternity.

As we long for and wend our way toward Homecoming, we are also called to move toward each other as marriage partners according to God's design for and Jesus' example of sacrificial love and glad submission. We have been given what we need to accomplish the task of obeying God's command to strive for restored balance in our marriages, and He invites us to discard our masks and learn to walk free with each other. Those husbands and wives who will accept the pain of His invitation will also find great joy in the journey. And when they get Home, it will be familiar.

QUESTIONS FOR THOUGHT AND DISCUSSION

1. How does each passage relate to our need for accountability relationships in marital healing?
>   Proverbs 13:10
>   1 Corinthians 12:7
>   James 5:16

2. What comfort can believing spouses take from these verses during the disruption of their change process?
>   James 1:2-5
>   1 Peter 4:12-19
>   1 Peter 5:6-7

3. Explain how Isaiah 61:1-3 and Jeremiah 29:11 can reassure us as we struggle to live without our masks.

4. How is God's intention stated in Romans 8:29 essential to our trust in Romans 8:28 as we pursue wholeness in our marriages?